Aquaponics

The Best Ways to Grow Aquaponic Plants

(Growing Your Food With Fish and Plants in a Closed-loop System)

William Cruz

Published By **Darby Connor**

William Cruz

All Rights Reserved

Aquaponics: The Best Ways to Grow Aquaponic Plants (Growing Your Food With Fish and Plants in a Closed-loop System)

ISBN 978-1-9992123-3-9

No part of this guidebook shall be reproduced in any form without permission in writing from the publisher except in the case of brief quotations embodied in critical articles or reviews.

Legal & Disclaimer

The information contained in this book is not designed to replace or take the place of any form of medicine or professional medical advice. The information in this book has been provided for educational & entertainment purposes only.

The information contained in this book has been compiled from sources deemed reliable, and it is accurate to the best of the Author's knowledge; however, the Author cannot guarantee its accuracy and validity and cannot be held liable for any errors or omissions. Changes are periodically made to this book. You must consult your doctor or get professional medical advice before using any of the suggested remedies, techniques, or information in this book.

Upon using the information contained in this book, you agree to hold harmless the Author from and against any damages, costs, and expenses, including any legal fees potentially resulting from the application of any of the information provided by this guide. This disclaimer applies to any damages or injury caused by the use and application, whether directly or indirectly, of any advice or information presented, whether for breach of contract, tort, negligence, personal injury, criminal intent, or under any other cause of action.

You agree to accept all risks of using the information presented inside this book. You need to consult a professional medical practitioner in order to ensure you are both able and healthy enough to participate in this program.

Table Of Contents

Chapter 1: Aquaponics One Zero One

The term Aquaponics is derived from a mixture of aquaculture, it is the manner of farming of fish and distinctive water species, and hydroponics, that is the system of developing vegetation without the need for soil. Both techniques are concerned in aquaponics.

In tremendous, the ordinary method of growing plant life in the outside is to dig soil in a garden bed, comply with plant fertilizer, sow seeds or plant seedlings, water the seeds, and watch them broaden. Aquaponics has the same purpose of developing vegetation; however, no soil is concerned and rather than the same old plant food or fertilizers, the fish offers the nutrients for the plant life.

This is to say that of the most important additives of aquaponics are the plants and the fish.

The vegetation and the fish are able to assist every one of a kind's health and increase given their natural trends and easy desires. The fish digests food and produces excrement this is launched into the water in which it swims. The excrement the fish produces is wealthy in substances that the plants require on the way to expand and convey.

Growing beds wherein the plant life are positioned permit the water to be allocated from the tank. As the flora extract the vitamins and the water they want for increase, additionally they smooth the water for the fish. There are stay micro organism at the growth mattress floor. These micro organism transform ammonia wastes that come from the fish into nitrates, which the plants can use. The technique of the ammonia conversion is called the nitrogen cycle.

The nitrogen cycle is one of the maximum widespread additives of the manner. As oxygen breaks down the ammonia into nitrates, the water movement takes away the nutrients that the fish does no longer want and transports them to the vegetation, who desires the ones nutrients. The water returning to the fish tank is then unfastened from nitrates that the fish does not need.

Thus, aquaponics is a form of food manufacturing tool with a win-win scenario. The fish gives meals for the flora at the identical time due to the fact the plant life provide clean water for the fish. It high-quality takes normal feeding of the fish, monitorial of water and its temperature, accurate pH and nitrate degrees, and well oxygenation of water for fish health.

An in Depth Look at the Nitrogen Cycle

The bacteria is one of the most critical elements of aquaponics. However, it's miles often least understood.

More frequently than now not, micro organism are classified as "germs", which might be awful. The truth is even though that micro organism also can be suitable.

In any type of large our bodies of water like a lake or ocean, fish excrete ammonia, it genuinely is diluted inside the water. However, while you maintain fish at domestic in smaller environments, ammonia desires to be moderated due to the fact it is quite poisonous to the fish. Ammonia additionally may be produced through food decomposition.

A few of the excessive outcomes of ammonia encompass the following:

Impairs the boom of the fish

Extensively damages tissues, which encompass the kidney and gills

Causes dying of the fish

Decreases the resistance of the fish to illnesses or deficiencies

Fortunately, Nitrosomonas sp, a exceptional bacterium, eats ammonia and converts it to nitrite. Nitrite is much less toxic to the health of the fish in assessment to the effect of ammonia. However, if left unmanaged, nitrate can prevent the fish from taking over oxygen.

On the opposite hand, Nitrobacter sp is a wonderful bacterium that eats nitrite, converting it to nitrate. Nitrate is favorable for the flowers as meals. The fish also can tolerate better nitrate stages than nitrite and ammonia. This is the nitrogen cycle.

Once the Aquaponics device reaches enough numbers of these micro organism to complete the conversion of ammonia to nitrites, the gadget is considered as having been "cycled."

Your primary cause is to set up the nitrogen cycle as speedy as you can, extending minimum stress on the fish and the plant life.

Bacteria will no longer be produced with out the respective meals of the aquatic existence you have got to your device. As such, you could see that ammonia tiers increase within the path of the tank installation. The micro organism will likewise increase or reproduce as an effect of developing the levels of ammonia. As speedy as ammonia is gift in the device, Nitrobacter sp will start to reproduce and artwork as fast as Nitrosomonas sp is generating nitrite.

Now that you have a smooth expertise of what aquaponic gardening is, allow's speak the benefits related to it.

10 Benefits of Aquaponics

There are some of treasured benefits or benefits why getting into this smooth and trouble-loose farming/gardening technique can be very ideal:

1. Produces surely natural meals.

Aquaponics has been stated to take organic to a higher diploma because of the truth you can not add any detail or chemical materials to the gadget that may damage or kill the fish. There isn't any want for chemical materials and as such, the meals you develop in an aquaponics garden is honestly herbal and free from any dangerous materials. Based on most medical researches, meals that has been grown organically consists of more extensive tiers of nutrients, vitamins, and minerals than food grown from conventional farming with chemical fertilizers. As such, you get meals this is herbal and wholesome.

2. Cleans and saves water.

Aquaponics makes use of ninety eight% less water in comparison to traditional farming. It is able to hold water as it recycles water in the tanks as an alternative of getting water sprayed in the course of fields with abandon as in traditional farming. Once the system is complete of water, you do now not want to refill and clean it. As water is sent, the vegetation extract the nutrients they need to expand and purifies the water on the same time through absorbing the fish waste that vegetation want so as to growth.

3. Can develop a massive kind of fish and plant species.

An aquaponics lawn can develop many types of fish and plants. You can pick out appropriate for eating fish kinds to develop into the system together with catfish, barramundi, tilapia, and trout among others. Many lovers of this tool have vouched that vegetation develop faster in aquaponics gardens, 10 instances as many given the same quantity of vicinity. Various herbs and veggies can develop on this gadget, which affords herbal produce. You best need to go out and select out what you want out of your aquaponics garden. If you really experience gardening, you can also choose ornamental plant and fish kinds to put in your device.

four. Operates in a hassle-loose and self-enough way.

Running an aquaponics lawn does not require unique competencies. You do no longer must be a pro to increase your very personal food on this tool. No hand weeding is vital. As prolonged as you apprehend its idea, you may installation your lawn and allow it run with the useful resource of itself in a closed tool. You will have it set up anywhere in your private home, within the residence or in the backyard. An aquaponics garden handiest dreams safety from very harsh climate and sufficient mild.

5. Embodies fee-effective farming/gardening.

As soon as you have got installation your lawn, the charges to run and keep it is probably very minimal. Aquaponic gardens do now not require chemical fertilizers, tool, or any specific tool to run. You do now not have to spend on system and tool for digging, watering, or weeding. Initially, you best need a fish tank, plastic cups or netting pots, water pumps, and plastic tubing to installation. Then, select your selected plant and fish kinds to place into the tool. To maintain, you excellent want a couple of minutes every day to ensure your lawn is running as anticipated. Ultimately, it'd most effective take a minimum amount of initial investment to set up an aquaponics lawn. A three hundred and sixty five days or less after that, you may find out that running and maintaining your lawn is type of free.

6. It's clean and cheaper to installation.

Unlike particular food production structures, aquaponics can be used by absolutely everyone with or without a historical beyond in farming, planting, or gardening. Aquaponics can be very clean to set up with only a marginal funding in terms of coins, time, and electricity. There is not any want for a huge vicinity or outdoor. Best of all, it does not require digging soil and buying fertilizers or one in all a type chemicals.

7. You will hold coins on food.

If you need to keep cash on meals, the awesome manner is to develop your private. Aquaponics can develop numerous types of both fish and greens. Moreover, you'll be assured that the meals produced via this approach is unfastened from poisonous chemicals. Aquaponics produces smooth, as well as nutritive, food in desire to most food to be had in the market that embody additives and chemicals.

eight. Your children can participate and study a precious life ability.

Even youngsters can take part in aquaponics. You can train your toddler on in which meals comes from via aquaponics as it consists of existence cycles of plants and fish. Aquaponics is likewise an super manner to teach children approximately traumatic for the flowers and the fish if you need to offer food.

9. It's a amazing interest.

Aquaponics is likewise best for the aged, retired human beings, or those with incapacity or infection. With handiest a touch help on putting in area the device, aquaponics may be finished as a sustainable hobby for livelihood or absolutely to combat boredom. For the elderly, retired humans, or human beings with incapacity or infection, the vegetation ought to be positioned at the ideal level or height just so there might be no need to bend or stretch at the same time as it's time to gain the vegetables. In terms of protection, it might handiest take so little time and effort to investigate the competencies and run the tool.

10. It takes little or no time to maintain.

Even if you are a busy man or woman or have a normal workplace interest, you could despite the fact that set up and function your very personal aquaponics garden. You quality need a hint a part of it gradual to preserve a tool. You may additionally even installation the device inner your property.

Let's skip immediately to the splendid styles of aquaponic systems.

Chapter 2: Media-Based Surely Or Gravel Bed System

The media-based aquaponics lawn is considered because the simplest kind to set up. It can be used in both domestic and commercial enterprise gardens. In reality, it is the maximum popular and typically utilized by lawn fanatics due to the reality it can keep the vegetation firmly; as a result, is ideal for developing various types of fruit-bearing flora.

This aquaponics tool uses boxes which is probably packed with small rocks of multiplied clay pebbles wherein the plant life increase. Expanded clay pebbles are usually used due to the fact they're able to absorb air and water effectively. The water from the tank is pumped into the media-stuffed beds in reality so the flowers benefit get right of get right of entry to to to the vitamins. The rocks function bio-filters that discard the want for introduced device.

In some instances, precise netted growing pots are used for the seeds. The pots in which the seeds are planted are complete of peat moss, clay pebbles, coir, or perlite. A large area complete of growing clay pebbles acts as receptacle for the pots in which the netted sides are absolutely included through the media.

Media-based aquaponics device may be operated in two techniques.

The first approach attracts off flowing water through the media mattress from the fish tank and again. The 2d method consists of a way called ebb and waft or flood and drain. In this technique, water is pumped into the growing beds to round 20130 centimeters in depth, and then, the water is tired based on a timer, which controls the cycle of flooding and draining.

Nutrient Film Technique (NFT)

This kind of aquaponics device is also usually used no matter the truth that not as lots as the media-based totally device.

In an NFT machine, water this is wealthy in nutrients is pumped into small gutters. The water flows very thinly into the enclosed gutters as that of a thin film. The plants are positioned in small netted pots or plastic cups just so their roots are capable of take in the water and its vitamins.

On the opportunity hand, NFT can simplest be used for particular plant species mainly green leafy vegetables with small to medium root structures. Plants having huge roots might be too heavy for the small enclosed gutters.

More often than now not, NFT is handiest utilized in big-scale aquaponics because of the fact it's miles pretty high-priced to set up. It uses mechanical filtration and PVC pipes to carry out. A bio-clean out is critical in order for bacteria to expand and undergo the nitrogen cycle. In addition, NFT also calls for solids filtration used for the solids in fish wastes. Solids filtration is commonly installation one at a time in a tank in which water passes prior to flowing through the PVC pipes.

Deep Flow/Deep Water Culture (DWC)/Raft

Deep drift or DWC aquaponics structures paintings thru the use of a foam raft, which floats at the water. This device is usually applied in commercial enterprise aquaponics despite the fact that it's also carried out in some outside aquaponics set ups. Most enterprise aquaponics pick out it over NFT due to the reality it is much less expensive to installation and control.

In deep float, a field is used for holding water, it surely is pumped from the fish tank after going through the nitrogen cycle. The plant life are placed within the raft with holes for his or her roots to cling within the water. Deep drift makes use of huge water volumes to offer robust temperatures of water for each the flora and the fish.

Many commercially-operated aquaponics use this tool because of the advantage it brings in terms of tending and harvesting the plant life. However, deep go along with the waft works better on leafy green veggies and herbs with small root systems than plant life and fruit sorts with massive root systems.

If deep go with the go with the glide is executed in home gardens, it uses a styrofoam tray that floats at the water of the fish tank. This tray has holes simply so the flowers can slump over the water. Some home gardens make use of netting pots wherein the roots can maintain and take in water. The fish sorts for deep float are maximum widely recognized to the ones that don't consume plants or plant roots.

In maximum commercially-operated aquaponics, deep go together with the drift operates with the aid of growing the fish in a tank and water is pumped the usage of a filtration device. The water flows in extended channels towards floating rafts with flora.

Regardless of the device to use, it's far useful to start small and constructing up on a larger scale later when you have enough capabilities and revel in. Let's now talk approximately all of the tool you want to get started out out with an aquaponic garden.

What Do You Need to Build an Aquaponics System?

An aquaponics system needs some fundamental additives to set up regardless of the type of system you choose. Depending on the amount of cash you are willing to spend, some variations for each issue also can have a look at.

The following are the essential additives for an aquaponics device set up:

1. Fish Tank

In installing an aquaponics tool, one of the most vital additives is a tank for the fish. The tank may be a meals-grade field, pool/pond, drum/barrel, or an aquarium. In reality, you can use something that might be able to maintain both water and the fish. The length of the tank relies upon on the shape of fish you desire to expand further to your choice to grow them as food or definitely be the vital part of your device.

2. Plant Trays

The trays for the flora will rely on the shape of device you need to set up. You can opt for Media-primarily based, NFT, or Deep Flow system. In massive, you'll want 1/2 of of barrels, PVC pipes or channels, rain guttering, Styrofoam sheets, and plastic bins or buckets. All the ones want to be deep sufficient just so they can be able to preserve 15 to 30 centimeters of water or developing medium.

3. Growing Medium

Like the plant trays, your developing medium also can be determined via manner of the form of tool you will use. All aquaponics structures do not require the use of soil. As such, you can need a few factor that might be able to guide the plants and preserve water.

four. Pumps

You will need every water and air pumps. The water pump is liable for water glide from the tank to the developing medium as a substitute to the tank. The air pump is answerable for air air glide within the tank. Air air drift is essential in an aquaponics machine because proper levels of oxygen are essential for each the fish and the flowers. The air pump works via absorbing air out of doors the machine and pushing such air into the water. In some instances, air stones are used in addition to an air pump to ensure the air bubbles are damaged aside for better oxygenation.

5. Plastic Tubing

In order to transport air and water to the device, you may want plastic tubing. Generally, air pumps employ zone-inch tubing while water pumps use half-inch tubing. Although plastic tubing is to be had in black and easy, it's far encouraged to use black tubing due to the truth it is able to keep algae from developing in addition to clogging the tube. Plastic tubing is less high-priced than individuals who you should purchase from aquarium deliver shops. In addition, plastic tubing is fairly durable.

6. Timer

Some systems necessitates for a time, that would keep track of the turning on and stale of the water pump. One of the structures that use a timer is an ebb and go along with the drift system, that could be a way utilized in a media-based totally aquaponics device. The timing for domestic aquaponics structures is commonly 1/2 of-hour increments.

7. Biological Filter

The need for a biological clean out or bio-clean out is based upon at the shape of tool you need to set up. Just like an aquarium, an aquaponics system wishes suitable bacteria just so unstable pollutants from the fish waste can be transformed to an lousy lot a lot less risky nitrates and nitrites. Although gravel is an powerful bio-clean out in your tank, it's miles viable that you could however need a separate bio-clear out. For example, having gravel inside the bottom of your fish tank can be a bio-clear out; but, you may have to accumulate the bacteria all yet again each time you easy the developing medium. As such, it's miles final to have a separate bio-clean out to keep away from taking on effort and time in building up micro organism.

8. Plants

There are many plant types that you can broaden in an aquaponics system. You can start off with a whole lot much less complex types which encompass leafy vegetables, along side silver beet, lettuce, and spinach, herbs, broccoli, and strawberries. The sort of plants that you could increase likewise relies upon on your form of device. According to maximum experts, developing root vegetables which includes radishes, potatoes, and carrots can even paintings nicely.

Chapter 3: Starting An Aquaponics System

Just like in constructing a residence or starting a business organisation, putting in an aquaponics device includes having a maintain near plan or blueprint of what you motive to achieve as an final outcomes. Once you have got had been given determined the goals to your device, you need to gather the device additives formerly stated.

The idea of aquaponics is getting a tool "cycling." This manner that you regularly need to installation beneficial micro organism populations inside your gadget for the micro organism to transform fish waste containing ammonia into nitrates and the plants can employ them.

There are severa strategies to start your device. Experts say that it is proper to "seed" your device from an present one. This suggests that your tool may want to come back from an already hooked up tool. Beneficial bacteria will fill aquarium filters. The equal is actual with pond filters and the water within the pond or aquarium. Thus, in case you are able to accumulate the micro organism from any other tool, putting in place your very very own system may be lots quicker.

On the alternative hand, you want not fear if there is no distinctive tool available. Bacteria will develop manifestly to your tool; however, it'll take a chunk at the identical time as. A take a look at bundle is usually recommended for following the cycle of your device.

A test kit accountable for attempting out pH, nitrate, nitrite, and ammonia may be a incredible help for monitoring your machine. Ideally, go away your gadget operational for at the least two days earlier than including fish to make certain that the device is operating as expected. Potential issues, together with leaks, may additionally arise. Make sure which you have resolved any issues in advance than the fish is placed into the tank.

There are severa techniques of biking, which includes:

1. Urea Fertilizers

This approach of cycling is straightforward and calls for sorting out the water frequently. Urea fertilizer is to be had in agricultural and hardware stores. Make positive that you placed urea fertilizers into your machine with the right amount. Otherwise, it could harm the fish and the flowers.

2. Feeder Fish/Fingerling

This is taken into consideration the only and quite advocated method of biking. The biking manner of your tool is done via adding feeder fish prior to together with your chosen fish species to broaden. Some of the most commonplace feeder fish species include goldfish and bronze comets.

You furthermore have the selection to inventory your device with fingerling of any fish species which you want to broaden on your device. When feeding the fish, you need to maintain as a minimum one tablespoon a day for each 500 liters of media for the primary   months. You have to save you feeding as soon as your device has an algae bloom until it clears. After more than one months, you can regularly growth feed stages for the cause that the micro organism has already set up inside the machine.

3. Dead Fish or Prawn

Although it is able to seem hard to trust, one of the oldest methods of cycling is adding useless or rotting fish or prawn inside the gadget. This induces a huge source of ammonia from which bacteria will feed.

four. Peeponics

Probably an weird method of cycling; but, a few people have their aquaponics system cycled thru which includes urine to it. This is due to the fact urine consists of urea, which breaks down into ammonia. Ammonia, then again, is a beneficial meals supply for micro organism. People who employ urine as a cycling technique for his or her structures allow urine to age for numerous days in a properly-ventilated open region.

five. Ammonia

This biking technique of setting ammonia in an aquaponics machine has been used broadly no matter the reality that not as commonplace as which consist of feeder fish and fingerling. Household ammonia can come from virtually one of a type places, but, in case you plan to use it as a biking approach it's miles important to display the quantity you install your gadget. In addition, quality food grade ammonia is authorized to be located in the device. Other commercial and cleaning ammonia assets have additives that might harm the fish and the flora.

6. Fish Feed

Many humans start their gadget with the useful resource of using using fish feed as a cycling approach. Once the feed starts to pick out the lowest of the fish tank, it releases ammonia, which the micro organism feed on. Fish feed also can damage down in the developing beds of your gadget.

Choosing a Good Location

One of the most essential subjects to maintain in mind is wherein to region your tool.

1. If you've got severa options for the vicinity of your device, recollect the only that can offer sufficient sunlight hours for it. For the flowers to increase nicely, they may need at least four to six hours of specific daytime on a every day basis. On the alternative hand, the fish do no longer want sunlight hours the least bit.

In reality, if sun is directed to your fish tank, it can result in algae bloom. Thus, it is top notch to preserve daylight far from the fish tank. This is the cause why we endorse the usage of placing or floating flowers in fish tanks to protect the fish or offer hiding locations for the fish from sunlight hours. The ground of the water can be a place to expand plants, which typically typically tend to fill your growing media.

2. Another factor to do not forget while deciding on a vicinity for your gadget is the get right of access to to strength or energy. Since you can need each water and air pump, you need to energy them a outstanding manner to run. You should ensure that your energy supply, further to the pumps, will not be wet with the useful resource of rain.

3. You additionally ought to make certain that you will be capable of plant, harvest, and preserve your tool in your chosen region. More regularly than no longer, as soon because the developing beds are already full of plant life, it is able to be difficult to get right of entry to the yet again part of the system. You want to make sure that the area you pick allows you to get right of get right of entry to to the entire device. You moreover want suitable get entry to to the fish tank so

that you can results use a fish internet to achieve your fish.

4. Since seasons exchange, ensure that the location is ideal for any season. For instance, if you have installation your tool at some stage in summer time, make sure that the location is still green at some point of wintry weather months.

5. Many fish deaths had been due to flora surrounding the machine. When choosing an area for your gadget, it is essential to don't forget that it is unfastened from plant infection, in particular from trees and shrubs. Fish deaths may be introduced about without issue via some flora or leaves of a surrounding tree or plant, which can be mainly poisonous.

6. Finally, you need to furthermore remember a vicinity this is stable no longer most effective on your gadget however for kids and pets as nicely. You need to make certain that your system is placed in a toddler-quality and pup-first-rate area to keep away from any form of accidents.

Choosing Your Growing Media

Different types of developing media are available for use in aquaponics systems. However, there are some factors to take into account on the identical time as deciding on the developing media to use.

First, it is most appropriate to apply a media that is amongst eight and sixteen millimeters. Anything past this range may additionally reason some negative outcome. For instance, in case you use a media this is appreciably smaller than the desired length, there can be minimum air space the numerous growing bed and the media. If you operate a bigger media than the famous size, the floor region may be reduced considerably and it is probably tough to plant.

You might also choose pea gravel or crushed river rock, as it's cheaper. It can but, be very heavy.

You may additionally moreover use four-16mm clay pebbles. This lasts for all time, does now not rot or break down, and could no longer grow fungus. Clay pebbles are heaps lighter than overwhelmed river rock and are a notable media choice to get your first aquaponic garden up and walking.

Chapter 4: Choosing Your Fish Species

In any aquaponics machine, the fish are very important. This is due to the fact they offer nutrients that the flora need that allows you to increase. If you are developing suitable for eating fish, they may moreover provide you with a splendid food supply.

Initially, you could locate that preserving fish may be a bit stressful especially if you do now not have in advance enjoy. However, you should no longer be disheartened. Keeping fish in an aquaponics gadget is really an awful lot less difficult compared to preserving them as aquarium fish. It all really boils all the way right right down to selecting the most suitable fish species after which growing them from fingerling to prepared to obtain fish.

When choosing the splendid fish to boom in your aquaponics tool, your primary attention is what your purpose is to your tool.

For example, you can pick out from safe to devour fish, collectively with tilapia or perch in case your reason for the device is to increase fish for intake. Otherwise, you may choose out a extra ornamental fish, along facet goldfish, in case you are the use of the fish simply for decor and to help your system.

Which fish species is most appropriate in your system? Let's check your alternatives for every suitable for eating and ornamental fish.

Edible Fish

1. Tilapia

This is one of the maximum cultured fish species inside the worldwide. It is ideal for aquaponics because it grows rapid, it's miles clean to reproduce, is right to eat, and consumes an omnivorous healthy eating plan. Tilapia calls for decent water to expand well. Thus, in case you live in a cool region, it is sincerely useful to develop fish this is extra appropriate for your weather.

2. Catfish

Around the area catfish has notable species which may be appropriate for aquaponics systems. In the united states, channel catfish is desired in maximum aquaculture settings. Catfish is likewise available in maximum areas in Australia. Catfish has a massive meals conversion ratio and is easy to enlarge.

three. Trout

If you stay in a place with cool temperature, trout is a notable fish species to apply for your aquaponics gadget. Trout prefers temperatures between 10°C and 20°C. Like catfish, trout moreover has nicely food conversion ratios and speedy increase charges.

4. Barramundi

During warmer months, barramundi is a exquisite fish to develop. Growers of this fish species buy mature inventory so that you can harvest huge fish due to the fact the developing season ends. Many those who want to consume fish have attested that barramundi grown in an aquaponics device is cleaner and crispier in flavor compared to standard techniques of farming this fish species.

Decorative Fish

1. Goldfish

Goldfish may be determined at any nearby home dog supply save and is also quality for an aquaponic lawn. They want plant cowl inside the fish tank as a way to breed.

2. Koi

Nowadays, Koi has grow to be very popular in Asian worldwide places that accept as proper with within the fortune this fish species can deliver. Koi are cute and may fit properly on your aquaponic garden.

There are unique fish species that you could use that may be available for your locality. For example, you may moreover comprise glowing water prawns, smooth water mussels, and sparkling water crayfish. Mussels are brilliant help for cleansing the water inside the fish tank because they may be clear out-feeders. Crustaceans also may be delivered.

If you're in a tropical region, you may opt for Red Claw, this is a native fish species in Australia. Red Claw has a totally fast growth charge. For cooler areas, you can use Yabbies. With the proper quantity of sunlight hours, suitable water temperature, and right environment, Yabbies can breed without troubles. They extend speedy although they're liable to cannibalism even as stocked densely.

Fish Quantity

When selecting the fish species you need to broaden to your aquaponics system, you moreover may also moreover need to don't forget the amount of fish you need. The amount of fish has added on a consistent debate amongst aquaponics fanatics. This is because of the fact there can be no unique type of fish to be placed in a system.

A favored tenet to conform with that most professionals advise is to stock about 20 to twenty-five fish for every 500 liters of growing media in a tool. This is primarily based on the assumption that the growing beds are about 25 to 30 centimeters deep.

The developing mattress consists of 250 liters of media, this is proper for 10 to 12 fish. This might allow the fish to boom from fingerling length to plate duration of about four hundred to 500 grams. If you are making the dimensions of the developing mattress two instances as hundreds due to the fact the particular, you could likewise double the huge style of fish to 20 to twenty-five fish.

However, the quantity of fish that you can hold on your machine is based upon of different factors, alongside aspect amount of flowers, feed fees, pumping costs, oxygen stages, water flows, water temperature, and fish species.

The reality is, your system and surroundings conditions may be unique to that of all of us else. Therefore, you need to examine the pointers and alter tiers in your specific situations and requirements. If generating fish for intake or feasible sale then it can be useful at the manner to growth the quantity of fish you inventory your system with.

However, it has been installed that the higher the stocking level, the better the tendency for things to head wrong. Heavy degrees of stocking require a keen eye on water parameters to make certain that the situations are on the most dependable kingdom. If you lower the ranges of fish stocking, you moreover may additionally lower the degrees of stress and threat. In most gently-stocked structures, the growth charges of plant life are speedy and wonderful.

Therefore, it's far vital to take small risks while stocking your first aquaponic system. Learn from your successes and disasters and adjust as a result.

Choosing Your Plants

There are numerous methods to start growing plant life for your aquaponics lawn.

First, is beginning from seed. With this approach you'll in reality sprinkle your seed of choice calmly all through the top of your growing media. This is a technique called broadcasting. This works properly for smaller seeds normally planted in the early spring, at the side of lettuce and carrots.

Plants that come from huge seeds will be predisposed to no longer germinate as well in an aquaponics device due to the fact the plant life of smaller seeds do. Therefore, you could want to try germinating those massive seeds from plant life, such as cucumbers, peas, and beans, first in a paper towel in advance than along with them to your device.

All you need to do is upload the seeds to a moist paper towel and seal it in a zipper lock bag. Sprouting have to rise up pretty rapid so take a look at them each day for a root. Once the inspiration has grown to at least 1 inch in length, definitely transfer them for your system and plant in your growing media. Roots want to be organized to that they will get wet at the identical time as planted.

Difficult to germinate vegetation, together with severa vegetables, and possibly peppers and tomatoes can be started out out directly in developing media and transferred to the gadget once they've started growing.

You can also use the roots of present flowers or seedlings you've got bought in your aquaponics lawn.

However, you do not must restriction your flowers to any character of those techniques. You could have a aggregate of seedlings, half of-grown flora, and mature plants on your gadget all at one time. With this, you may be capable of cycle thru the flowers. Once the mature ones are removed, you can plant new ones for replacement. It is vital, even though, to have as many flowers as possible growing at one time to revel in the nutrients given off through manner of the fish.

With such numerous techniques to begin your lawn you should be capable of broaden a tremendous style of vegetation. Let's now speak which plant life you can choose out to expand.

It is fantastic to have a giant blend of plant species for your device. You should boom every decorative and not unusual residence plants on the side of plants which will produce food, which incorporates greens and herbs.

Listed under are a list of plant life as a way to increase nicely in any form of aquaponics device:

Pak Choi

Arugula

Mint

Spinach

Basil

Leafy lettuce

Chives

Watercress

Common residence plant life

Some flora that have better dietary dreams but can nevertheless be covered for your lawn:

Peppers

Beans

Squash

Tomatoes

Cucumbers

Peas

Below is a useful guide that will help you decide the type of plant to apply all through one in every of a kind seasons:

Spring (March, April, May)

Artichoke

Beans

Garlic

Herbs

Okra

Onions

Spinach

Squash

Cantaloupe

Carrots

Kale

Kohirabi

Parsley

Parsnips

Strawberries

Turnips

Summer (June, July, August)

Beans

Chard

Herbs

Lettuce

Okra

Peppers

Squash

Tomatoes

Corn

Garlic

Mustard vegetables

Onions

Spinach

Raddish

Fall (September, October, November)

Beetroot

Bok choy

Cauliflower

Celery

Lettuce

Mustard

Spinach

Sugar peas

Broccoli

Carrots

Kale

Peas

Radish

Turnips

Winter (December, January, February)

Asparagus

Beetroot

Endive

Horseradish

Parsley

Parsnips

Spinach

Turnips

Cabbage

Onions

Shallots

Peas

Chapter 5: Aquaponics Garden Guidelines

Once you've got finished the ones steps to installation your aquaponics tool, the subsequent step is to run and hold it.

There isn't any actual precise step-via the usage of-step method in running an Aquaponics tool. As rapid as you have built your machine, it can run via way of itself maximum of the time.

However, right here are a list of popular pointers so that it will consider while retaining your garden:

1. Make high-quality to preserve feed enter into your aquaponics device noticeably normal.

This can be carried out in approaches.

A. The first method is using staggered manufacturing and severa fish-rearing tanks. Take as an example an aquaponics tool with tilapia as its fish species. Generally, it'd have four rearing tanks and the production cycle might also take 24 weeks. The tilapia may additionally have great levels of boom in every rearing tank. Thus, you could harvest tilapia from one tank every 6 weeks. Once you harvest and restock with fingerlings, the general feed enter of your aquaponics device may also drop with the resource of manner of about 25% to 30%. On the opportunity hand, the overall feed input need to increase step by step to most in a span of 6 weeks.

The fluctuation inside the feed input as well as vitamins ranges is ordinary. If you only have one rearing tank for your machine, the feed enter ought to decline by means of manner of manner of as heaps as 90% throughout harvest and restocking and increase step by step to maximum in a span of 24 weeks. In addition, the nutrient levels could additionally be low upon stocking and immoderate for the duration of harvest. As such, it could stop result to awful widespread overall performance of your device.

B. The 2nd approach entails stocking one fish rearing tank with numerous duration businesses of your fish species. For example, if you use tilapia with a 6-month boom length, the rearing tank ought to at least have 6 agencies of fish in precise sizes. Every month you will dispose of the maximum crucial fish using a grader bar, that is pulled through the rearing tank.

After every partial harvest, you need to restock the rearing tank with an identical wide variety of fingerlings. Although the feed enter ration fluctuates, it might be bearable in every month-to-month cycle.

2. Make nice to allow top aeration.

In order to make certain most growth and fitness of the fish, the vegetation or maybe micro organism in your system, adequate ranges of dissolved oxygen is important. At least 5 mg/liter of dissolved oxygen degrees must be maintained in rearing tanks as well as inside the water circling the roots of the flowers. It is also crucial to have ok dissolved oxygen levels for maintain healthful populations of bacteria within the course of the nitrogen cycle. Chemical changes in some unspecified time in the future of the nitrogen cycle wherein ammonia and nitrite are converted to non-toxic nitrate need the proper quantity of oxygen for a successful method.

3. Make sure to place into effect natural manipulate.

Many therapeutants that address fish diseases and parasites are dangerous to beneficial micro organism, the flora, and the fish on your device. Pesticides that manipulate plant illnesses and manipulate insects are likewise toxic to the fish. In reality, there aren't any pesticides that have been authorised for meals fish use. Thus, therapeutants and pesticides should not be utilized in an aquaponics tool. The simplest choice you've got got a superb way to fight illnesses and manage bugs is through natural manage. This consists of the implementation of vast manipulate practices for stopping parasite troubles and sicknesses from going on inside the first location.

4. Make satisfactory to govern pH levels.

pH is pertained due to the truth the master variable as it's far answerable for controlling one-of-a-kind great variables in water. One of the most large variables in an aquaponics machine is the nitrification stage in the nitrogen cycle. Nitrification involves the conversion of ammonia and nitrite to nitrate. As the conversion occurs, the pH continuously decreases due to acid-producing technique. Thus, pH need to be measured on a every day basis and potassium and calcium hydroxide need to be delivered for acid neutralization.

In addition, pH impacts the solubility of vitamins. The best pH for solubility of nutrients is 6.Five or marginally decrease. You want to make certain that nitrification and solubility of vitamins meet at a positive level. Thus, it is enormously recommended that pH degree on your device is ready 7.0.

There are 4 subjects that might arise if the pH level will become too low.

First, the flowers can also additionally additionally have nutrient deficiencies. Second, boom and manufacturing of each the plant life and the fish decrease. Third, the nutrient separates itself from the solution. Finally, ammonia builds up and becomes poisonous to the fish and a new set of nutrients precipitate from the answer, having the same dangerous effects for the boom and production of the flora.

five. Make positive to use a feeding charge ratio for the calculations of your aquaponics gadget's design.

If you have got an as it ought to be designed aquaponics tool, the ration among the fish and the flora is dependent on the feeding charge ratio. The feeding price ratio refers to the amount of feed which you feed your fish on a every day basis steady with rectangular meter of the flowers' growing location. If your gadget is raft, the right ratio is between 60 and one hundred g/m²/day. For example, if you feed the fish with 1,000 g/day, you should have a place of 16.7 m² for plant production. That is, the feeding price ration is 60 g/m²/day.

On the alternative hand, if you have a plant production area of hundred m², the tank volumes, fish tanks, manufacturing schedules, and fish stocking costs need to be controlled to attain an average each day feed enter of 20,000 g based totally totally on a feeding rate ratio of one hundred g/m²/day. The best feeding charge ratio is counting on different factors together with the vegetation you expand, the hydroponic tool you operate, the share of water out of location in the end of the elimination of solids, and the supply water's chemical composition.

6. Make super to complement the species with potassium, calcium, and iron.

In order for the flora to increase, they want thirteen kinds of nutrients. Generally, fish feed gives 10 vitamins in truthful quantities.

On the opposite hand, potassium, calcium, and iron levels in an aquaponics device are typically too low to gain great plant growth. Therefore, they must be supplemented. More frequently than not, potassium and calcium are supplemented through which include simple compounds that regulate pH levels, which encompass potassium hydroxide and calcium hydroxide. Meanwhile, chelated compound is added to supplement iron.

7. Make notable to get rid of solids.

It is anticipated that about 25% of fish feed placed in a tool is discharged as sturdy waste and will boom primarily based completely mostly on moist weight. Thus, it's far advocated to cast off robust wastes from the system by means of the use of filtering or settling earlier than those wastes enter the hydroponic issue. Otherwise, the ones strong wastes will decrease stages of oxygen when they decay. This may additionally moreover additionally extensively have an effect on each the water and vitamins within the tool. If there are too many solids in the gadget, it'll have an large effect at the nitrification of micro organism. In addition, as soon as the solids decay oxygen decreases and yields ammonia.

8. Make advantageous to put in force correct enough bio-filtration.

Once the solids are removed, the subsequent step is bio-filtration. Bio-filtration is the system of ammonia oxidation to nitrate through nitrifying micro organism. If you have got a machine that makes use of nutrient movie method, the hydroponic issue has a bargain plenty much less floor vicinity to connect nitrifying bacteria; hence, bio-filters are vital. Bio-filters may be utilized in structures particularly if the fish species calls for superior incredible of water. In addition, bio-filters can improve safety elements for fish species which might be sensitive or lots much much less hardy.

Chapter 6: Troubleshooting

As with whatever else, there may be generally the capability for problems to upward thrust up indoors your aquaponic lawn.

First, it's miles fairly encouraged to have a backup gadget for at the same time as the power might possibly exit. Without energy to your aerator, your fish will now not remaining too lengthy due to the truth they consume the dissolved oxygen available in the water. As such, you want to be prepared with a way for the oxygen to get into the water that doesn't require power.

It is usually recommended that you maintain an aerator available that is battery operated. You may also use a generator in case the energy goes out.

On the opportunity hand, there might be an instance wherein the energy goes out and you are not domestic to expose on battery operated aerators or generators. Fortunately, you have got alternatives for an automatic backup device.

First, you can employ an AC/DC aerator. An AC/DC aerator is an air pump with integrated rechargeable batteries. More frequently than now not, AC/DC aerators run on the same time as they may be plugged in a electricity outlet. They pump air via air stones and air streams within the tank. Once the electricity is out, these aerators turn on robotically to their included batteries. Thus, they keep pumping air into the water. The lifestyles of the included batteries of AC/DC aerators usually lasts up to 10 hours. As soon as energy is once more, it switches again to the usage of power and the integrated batteries are recharged.

The 2d technique to have an automated backup device is to apply air or water pumps run by means of batteries. You can use an inverter, a power fail switch, automobile battery, or trickle battery to run an air pump or water pump. This sort of backup device works the identical way as the AC/DC aerators. However, that is larger and has individualized components. For example, you can separate and trade this tool by means of using the use of 12/24V DC additives and bypass over the inverter.

Several processes are to be had to deal with troubles that might rise up from pests, sicknesses, and one-of-a-kind deficiencies to your aquaponic device.

If your machine is pestered with sap sucking bugs, you may rent garlic and chili sprays, which is probably commercially to be had. However, you need to make sure which you use them moderately to keep away from harming or risking the fitness of the fish and the plants.

If molds and fungus, which generally harms plants, are the troubles to your device, you may hire potassium bicarbonate. However, you need to excellent spray them onto the plant life suffering from the molds and fungus.

There also are numerous procedures to address plant deficiencies. You can use each seaweed extracts or chelated iron for supplementation.

Safety Rules

There are numerous topics to preserve in mind regarding safety even as beginning and retaining your aquaponic lawn.

1. Water Risk

Open water ought to constantly be included as pets and youngsters can also get into the water.

2. Top Up Water Supply

A timer is usually recommended to hold handy even as filling your device so you apprehend even as to reveal the pumps on and rancid. That manner you save every water and power. It is vital not to overfill the tank as it can reason fish deaths due to low tiers of oxygen within the water. More so, when you have relatively chlorinated tap water, it can kill bacteria populations that boom within the growing beds. Tap timers are with out issues available and relatively cheap.

three. Power Supplies

Always make sure that you located electricity protection on your precedence list. Air and water pumps require energy resources; consequently, you want to shield them via an RCD. When you dip your hands into the water with the pump, you want to make certain that the pump is grew to turn out to be off. The leads need to be well-protected. They have to no longer get within the manner of preferred get admission to. Electrical gadgets which includes air pumps want to be saved out of rain and water. It is by no means a notable idea to go away an air pump sitting on pinnacle of the tank in which it can be knocked within the tank.

4. All Things Should be Kept Safe

Everything which you use for your aquaponics tool need to be saved in appropriate areas. Hazards together with fish feed should be locked as a lot as maintain secure from children and vermin.

Book Excerpt (How to Make Your Own Compost)

Benefits of Making Your Own Compost

When you begin to manufacture your very personal compost and use it to scenario the soil that your plant life are growing in you may start to understand many capability benefits.

1. Save Money

Composting your home's herbal wastes can lessen your rubbish extent with the resource of as masses as 75%.

You drastically lessen the quantity of waste substances from each your kitchen, your lawn and your out of doors. Instead of throwing out kitchen scraps or tediously amassing grass cuttings into luggage and looking ahead to the ones to be accumulated via the rubbish disposal people, you may truly add your devices on your compost pile, or flip these into mulch to your large vegetation. You can also upload recyclable materials like newspapers and unique paper merchandise into your compost.

Reducing the extent of your own family's waste materials can save you loads of cash in phrases of garbage series costs. There are a few states that price you a high-quality quantity regular with garbage bag; while different places fee you based mostly on the quantity and weight of the garbage they collect from your property.

Organic fertilizers and soil conditioners are often 25% to one hundred% greater costly than the monetary however synthetic/chemical-primarily based products, which you must not be the usage of the least bit.

Creating your personal fertilizers and soil conditioners can save you some of coins, especially when you have a nicely-tended garden, an indoor herb plot, or an expansive outside.

Using natural compost to your flora, garden or backyard additionally improves the soil's moisture absorption functionality.

This manner that the earth maintains water longer. Therefore, you may moisten your patch of land less frequently, or with a lot much less amount of water. This holds right for big gardens or yards, or regions that generally enjoy immoderate, humid, or dry climates. Using plenty much less water for gardening translates to hundreds of financial economic financial savings on your water bill.

2. Protect the Environment

Composting will lessen your property's garbage extent.

Reducing waste is normally better for the surroundings. Aside from the reality that you located a lot much less stress on Mother Nature's final herbal assets, you moreover might also right now recycle natural materials which allows reduce global warming.

Less rubbish on a each day foundation moreover interprets to much less garbage within the landfills. This would possibly help lessen down the quantity of methane gasoline and unique toxic emissions from said regions that make contributions to the deterioration of the the earth's ozone layer.

On the identical have a look at, you assist amplify the lifestyles of modern landfills, and might even prevent or put off the want to create new ones.

You reduce the amount of leachate within the landfills via turning your herbal wastes into compost.

Organic substances regularly produce leachate, liquid which contains doubtlessly dangerous substances from substances thru which it has exceeded, that might contaminate every ground and ground water, now not to say the soil wherein it's far located.

Organic fertilizers and soil conditioners are generally better for the soil.

They offer vegetation and other microorganisms the vitamins they want with out artificially or negatively effecting the herbal balance of the soil. More importantly, these products degrade organically which creates a cleanser and additional secure environment.

Using compost in your garden or backyard helps loosen clay soil and promotes better drainage during the plant roots.

This permits your vegetation to expand faster due to the nutrient-rich addition to the pinnacle soil. Plus, your floras' roots have greater area to unfold out. Once your flowers' roots are properly anchored, this lessens the opportunity of soil erosion.

three. Improve Your Health

Composting does not create air pollutants (inclusive of these created through burning).

Air pollutants can motive hypersensitive reactions attacks, bronchitis, or extraordinary lung-associated troubles. Composting is 100% better than burning your garden cuttings and outdoor trimmings.

Using compost yields greater healthful and faster growing plants that, in flip, gives us clean air.

Flora which encompass the ones system the carbon inside the environment and launch smooth, breathable oxygen as a derivative. This allows reduce down the quantity of smog and carbon emissions, specially in business regions, or places close to factories and manufacturing vegetation.

Using your very very own compost is natural and herbal and gets rid of the need to apply chemical fertilizers and conditioners on your plants, that have been established to negatively have an impact for your fitness.

Eating food grown the use of chemical fertilizers can motive you to become sick or maybe boom a number of cancers. Simply entering repeated contact with the chemical fertilizers can do the same.

Tending in your compost is right bodily interest.

The smooth act of turning the compost pile over will will let you burn off as masses as 350 electricity in an hour and hold all of your essential fats urning hormones in balance.

How to Start Your Freestanding Compost Pile

One of the best methods of beginning your non-public composting efforts is to create a freestanding, cardio compost pile. The first component you have to keep in mind is wherein to vicinity this.

An satisfactory spot may be out returned, nicely away from the same antique paths of interest of your home. This may help prevent your circle of relatives individuals or pets from stumbling on your compost heap with the aid of the use of twist of fate. This moreover prevents it from becoming an eyesore to your panorama.

In wonderful areas, it's far unlawful to create home compost piles which is probably without a doubt visible from the street. So it can pay to test up on community housing legal guidelines in your location in advance than you pick out a gap.

You need to choose an area this is quite shaded or sheltered. This may reduce the possibility of the compost pile being laid low with drastic modifications inside the weather. For instance, a sudden gust of sturdy wind may blow away loose fragments of compost, rain might possibly soak the whole compost pile through, or a shocking drop in temperature may also freeze the pile wherein it stands.

You want enough elbow area to transport approximately. This shape of composting would possibly want everyday turning. This can't be achieved correctly if you are going for walks in a decent area.

Chapter 7: Why Should You Consider Aquaponics

Aquaponics is an interesting subject for anyone looking to grow their own plants with the benefit of using fish as the nutrient source. A system can be as small as to have one on your kitchen bench using goldfish and growing herbs. To a larger system in your yard with silver perch growing lettuces, tomatoes, herbs etc. An aquaponics system is made up of a tank containing the fish, and one or more grow beds for vegetable production.

The fish supply nutrients to the plants that are in a grow bed and the plants clean the water of the nutrients and the water then travels back into the fish tank creating a recirculating system. The fish water is pumped to the grow bed/s, using a system of pipes. The grow bed can be filled with gravel (flood and drain), clay pebbles or water (continuous flow). The fish water feeds the plants of which there is a huge range to choose from to plant such as tomatoes, cucumbers, lettuce and green leafy vegetables, the water then returns to the fish tank preferably by gravity. The water that is returned to the fish tank is clean and ready for use by the fish, and so the cycle continues.

Aquaponics is suitable for a number of fish such as Barramundi, Bass, Jade Perch, Golden Perch, Silver Perch, Murray Cod if you are in Australia all of which are great to eat as well. Tilapia is the most common fish used in an aquaponics system outside of Australia.

So we have established that water is recirculated through the system, and you will need to add a small amount of water to compensate for what is lost by evaporation, and transpiration by the vegetables. Therefore aquaponics uses only about 10% of the water required for traditional gardening or fish farming. Aquaponics is the future of home gardening and commercial fresh food production for any country.

Aquaponics is a balanced, self-contained eco system that works!! No chemicals are added or for that matter can be added to the vegetable part of the system as that would cause your fish to die. Garden pests can be kept to a minimum by housing the system in a green house or by using non toxic methods.

Aquaponics is a highly sustainable method of Agriculture. There is some input and maintenance with aquaponics system such as cleaning filters and feeding the fish. The primary benefits to aquaponics are:

1 Environmentally responsible with low water usage and low power usage.

2 The primary inputs to the system are Fish food and water.

3 Little to no Chemical usage. Aquaponics requires no synthetic fertilizers and few pesticides.

4 Many of the plants that thrive in aquaponics growing are very easy to grow.

5 Low susceptibility to pests and diseases

6 Timely crop turn around

7 Increased crop production per square foot versus traditional farming

8 Multiple crops and fish can be grown from the same system

9 Fish can be harvested as an additional food or revenue source

Aquaponics has become increasingly popular as a growing system in the past 10 years.

Much of this growth has been due to how sustainable and environmentally friendly aquaponics is. Food production takes center stage when discussing ways to become not only more environmentally responsible but also when promoting healthy eating and supporting local members of our community. More people are turning to aquaponics to teach our future generations about sustainability, build healthy local businesses and take control of their food source every day.

At the forefront of aquaponics benefits is its ability to grow several types of food while consuming very few resources in the process. Power is needed to operate a system but there are few pieces of equipment that require power. This leads to a low net power usage.Even less water is used as most aquaponics systems are recirculating, meaning water is circulated through the system rather than disposed of after use. The primary water loss in aquaponics comes from evaporation and plant transpiration, accounting for very little loss.

Equally important is that in many systems the need for pesticides and other chemicals is low, and is sometimes not needed at all. Aquaponics systems were designed for use in a controlled environment, like a greenhouse or indoor warehouse, so exclusion is the pest management practice most widely used. The process of bacteria converting fish waste to plant food, or nutrients, eliminates the need for fertilizer. Even pH is adjusted on its own within the system through the process of bacteria converting the fish waste.

You're not trying to replicate nature as much as you are letting it flourish in aquaponic tanks. Nature does its work by creating an environment in the system where fish and plants thrive. Our part is to introduce the participants and let them find their balance. A watchful eye is key because variables outside of the aquaponics system or the greenhouse can create problems. This includes power outages and extreme temperatures, but aside from these aquaponics systems are self-correcting.

Aquaponics systems are a simple way to grow food. Minimal maintenance is needed and the main efforts are in feeding the fish, seeding new crops and harvesting. Once the system is running, the primary task day to day is feeding the fish and checking for signs that the balance of the system is changing. Monitoring water chemistry, temperature, and nutrient levels and moving to correct them as needed will keep an Aquaponics system thriving.

The simplicity doesn't take away from actual vegetable or floriculture production volume. At a rate of 4-5 times faster, in terms of crop turns, when compared to traditional farming, aquaponics systems can hold their ground. Not only is the crop turn speedier but the density of planting is also increased.

One of the most interesting features of an aquaponics system is its conduciveness to polyculture. Fruiting and leafy vegetables can be grown side by side. Fish and plants are being harvested from one system. There are many options as for what can be grown using aquaponics growing systems. Not only are the plant options wide there are also a decent number of fish species that will grow in a system.

CAN A COMMERCIAL AQUAPONICS GREENHOUSE BE PROFITABLE?

This is a common question that circulates in forums, and for good reason. Aquaponics is a more sustainable method of growing than conventional agriculture, but if it's not financially sustainable as well, it is not a viable venture for most growers. Before we evaluate data on this question, two caveats. First, growers' expected financial returns vary greatly. Some operations are non-profits, just trying to break even. Others want to be large-scale agricultural businesses with significant returns. As a first step, it's important to identify your goals when evaluating profitability. We explain this more in Planning a Commercial Aquaponics Greenhouse.

Thesecond caveat is that everyoperation is different. No onecan make definitiveclaims about whether an individual aquaponics greenhouse will be profitable. As one member noted in the forum Year-Round Greenhouse Growers, asking whether an aquaponics greenhouse business will beprofitable is just likeasking if a car dealership will beprofitable, it depends. Toplan for your business specifically, we recommend taking a course or using the manyavailable resources to help you plan for your unique commercial aquaponics venture.

Most growers understand this intuitive point.Rather than asking about a specific operation, they want to know about the industryoverall. Is commercial aquaponics a safe industry to go into? Areother aquaponics greenhouses profitable, and what do those businesses look like?

In regards to these questions, a 2014 study from Johns Hopkins University can shed some light. The study surveyed 257 commercial aquaponics growers, most located in the US. It tallied many metricsabout their operation and some metrics on financial success. Some of key findings:

1 Most operations use an aquaponics greenhouse, often in addition toanother structure

2 The averagesize of the operations is .03 acres (1,307 sq. ft.). About 40% of operations are located at the growers home; the remainder were on commercial or agricultural zoned land.

3 Most growers used a combination of two or more aquaponics systems (media beds, wicking beds, rafts, nutrient film technique, and vertical towers), with rafts and media beds being the most common.

4 The median year that respondents had begun practicing aquaponics was 2010.

5 31% of respondents were profitable in thepast year.

6 55% expected to beprofitable within the next 12 months and most growers (75%) expected to be profitable in the next 36 months.

7 For 70% of respondents, their commercial aquaponics operation was not the primary sourceon income. The data above shed some light on whether commercial aquaponics industry in the US is profitable overall. With onlyabout 1/3 of growers stating that their operation profitable, it'sclear that commercial aquaponics is not a safe bet or an assuredly profitable industry. However, it's important

toput this number in context. Most operationsare still in thestart-upphase, with an average time in businessof about 4 years at the time of the study. Furthermore, thestudy did not ask about growers' intention/goals. One can deduce from the majorityof growers who do not make aquaponics their primary profession that thesurvey includes somecommercial growers whoprobably don't need or want to make significant profits. Profitabilitystatistics would likely change if it evaluated only those who made a living from their commercial aquaponics greenhouse. It'salso important to note thereare many things a grower can do to increase thechances of success. The Johns Hopkins Study noted that several traits related toprofitability:

Sell a varietyof products

The study notes that a commercial aquaponics operation was more likely to be profitable if it sold other products and services in addition toplantsand fish. The study did not specify these auxiliary services, but examples likely include other agricultural products or services like consulting and courses.

More knowledge

The study confirms a fairly obvious idea that growers who have a strong knowledge of aquaponics are more likely to be profitable. For this reason, i often recommend growers start out with an introductory business planning and/or growing course in commercial aquaponics, by reading the below contents h

osted .

Chapter 8: Basics Of Aquaponics

They say one person's trash is another's treasure.The day-old bagels a franchise views as too stale for customers taste perfectly delicious to the hungry when they're distributed at a homeless shelter. The annoying, hyperactive puppy one family abandons at the dog pound because it chews shoes becomes another family's rambunctious little delight. What one group sheds as waste, another takes in as nourishment. It's a lovely circle.

With aquaponics, this same circle is turning -- only it doesn't have anything to do with bagels or puppies. Aquaponics is a method of cultivating both crops and fish in a controlled environment. The fish are kept in tanks, and the plants are grown hydroponically -- meaning without soil. They sit in beds, but their roots hang down into a tub of water. When fish live in tanks, their waste builds up in the water, and it eventually becomes poisonous to them. But what is toxic for fish is nourishing for plants -- they love nothing more than to suck down some fish waste. So with aquaponics, the fish waste-laden water from the fish tanks is funneled to the tubs where the plants dangle their roots. When the plants absorb the nutrients they need from that water, they basically cleanse it of toxins for the fish. Then that same cleansed water can be funneled back into the fish tanks.

This method of farming fish and crops is a good thing on several different levels. First of all, it removes fertilizer and chemicals from the agricultural process. The fish waste acts as a natural fertilizer for the crops, instead. Second of all, it saves water because the water is recycled within the tanks rather than sprayed across a field of crops with abandon. Thirdly, an aquaponics environment can be set up anywhere, so it reduces the need for local communities to import fish and crops from other countries. That saves fuel -- also a positive.

aquaponics, with its fancy name, may sound like a trendy new concept developed by environmentalists. But it's actually as old as the hills.The origins of aquaponics can be traced to ancient Egyptian and Aztec cultures.The ancient Aztecs developed chinampas, man-made floating islands, which consisted of rectangular areas of fertile land on lake beds.Aztecs cultivated maize, squash and other plants on the chinampas and fish in the canals surrounding them. The fish waste settled on the bottom of the canals, and the Aztecs collected the waste to use as fertilizer [source: Growfish]. Additionally, countries in the Far East like Thailand and China have long used aquaponics techniques in rice paddies. Let's learn how this ancient farming method is applied today.

Cultivating plants and fish through aquaponics is both easy on the environment and easy on finances. Aquaponics systems don't use any chemicals, and they require about 10 percent of the water used in regular farming. The systems are closed -- that is, once they've been filled with water, only a small amount is introduced into the system thereafter to replace evaporated water. But how can a water-based system use less water than conventional farming?

The answer is the continual reuse and recycling of water through naturally occurring biological processes. Basically, the waste from fish produces natural bacteria that converts waste like ammonia into nitrate. This nitrate is then absorbed by plants as a source of nutrients. The basic principle of aquaponics is to put waste to use.

Let's take a look at the step-by-step process:

Fish living in aquaponics tanks excrete waste and respirate ammonia into water. Ammonia is toxic to fish in high concentrations, so it has to be removed from the fish tanks for fish to remain healthy.

Ammonia-laden water is processed to harvest helpful types of bacteria such as Nitrosomonas and Nitrobacter. Nitrosomonas turns ammonia into nitrite, while nitrobacter converts into nitrate.Both of these nitrates can be used as plant fertilizer.

Nitrate-rich water is introduced to the hydroponically grown plants (plants grown without soil). These plants are placed in beds that sit on tubs filled with water, and the water is enhanced by the nitrate harvested from the fish waste. The plants' bare roots hang through holes in the beds and dangle in the nutrient-laden water.

The roots of the plants absorb nitrates, which act as nutrient-rich plant food. These nitrates, which come from fish manure, algae and decomposing fish feed, would otherwise build up to toxic levels in the fish tanks and kill the fish. But instead, they serve as fertilizer for the plants.

The hydroponic plants' roots function as a biofilter -- they strip ammonia, nitrates, nitrites and phosphorus from the water. Then, that clean water is circulated back into the fish tanks.

Because fish waste is used as fertilizer, there's no need for chemical fertilizers. The money and energy it would take to put those chemicals to work is saved. In fact, the only conventional farming method that's used to operate an aquaponics system is feeding the fish.

Now you know how aquaponics works on a biochemical level. But which kinds of fish are best for these systems? And which plants thrive in them? Let's find out.

Many warm-water and cold-water fish species have been adapted to aquaponics systems. The most commonly cultivated fish in aquaponics systems are tilapia, cod, trout, perch, Arctic char and bass. But out of all of these, tilapia thrives best. Tilapia are very tolerant of fluctuating water conditions, such as changes in pH, temperature, oxygen and dissolved solids. They also are in high demand -- this white-fleshed fish is frequently sold in markets and restaurants.

Which plants thrive well in aquaponics systems? That depends on the density of the fish tanks and the nutrient content of the fish waste. In general, the best plants to cultivate in an aquaponics system are leafy greens and herbs. The high-nitrogen fertilizer generated through fish waste allows plants to grow lush foliage. So, leafy plants tend to flourish in aquaponics systems. Lettuce, herbs and greens like spinach, chives, bok choy, basil, and watercress have low to medium nutritional requirements and usually do well in aquaponics systems.

Plants yielding fruit have higher nutritional requirements, and although they grow well in aquaponics systems, they need to be placed in systems that are heavily stocked and well established. Vegetables like bell peppers, cucumbers and tomatoes can be cultivated in these types of aquaponics systems. The only plants that don't seem to respond as well are root crops like potatoes and carrots. Without soil, these crops wind up misshapen, and they're hard to harvest properly.

Aside from plants and fish, the other major component of aquaponics is the water itself.That said, carefully monitoring the water's pH, which determines acidity, is of the upmost importance to ensure safe levels for the fish. Water quality testing e?uipment is very important to ensure that both fish and plants remain healthy. It's also important to keep an eye on dissolved oxygen, carbon dioxide, ammonia, nitrate, nitrite and chlorine. The density of the fish in the tanks, the growth rate of the fish and the amount of feed they're given can produce rapid changes in water quality, so careful monitoring is important. Although the ratio of fish tank water to hydroponic product depends on fish species, fish density, plant species and other factors, a general rule of thumb is a ratio of 1:4 tank contents to bed contents. Basically, for every one part of water and fish, you'll want to have four parts plant and bed material.

Some aquaponics systems are outfitted with biofilters, living materials that naturally filter pollutants out of water and that facilitate the conversion of ammonia and other waste products. Other systems feed fish waste directly into the hydroponic vegetable beds.

Gravel in the vegetable bed acts has a bioreactor, a material that helps carry out the chemical processes of living organisms. The gravel does this by both removing dissolved solids and providing a place for the nitrifying bacteria to convert into plant nutrients.

Want to bring food production into your backyard? Read on to learn how to set up your own aquaponics system.

Aquaponics systems are definitely a force on the larger industrial and commercial food production scene. But in reality anyone can implement aquaponics basics into their backyard gardening. Whether you set up a system on your patio, your apartment roof or in your backyard, a properly operating aquaponics system can provide food for an entire family.

It'd be pricy to set up a full-scale, commercial-sized aquaponics system. But backyard gardeners can set up an inexpensive aquaponics system using recycled materials. For the backyard vegetable gardener, aquaponics can offer many benefits. These systems use much less water than a conventional garden, and you won't lose much water through evaporation. Your plant harvest definitely will be organic because you can't use chemicals -- they'd harm your fish. Additionally, aquaponically farmed vegetables grow much faster that those grown in a conventional garden. It's been reported that cucumbers can be harvested in as few as 25 days when seedlings are transplanted from a conventional garden to an aquaponics system [source: Growfish].

What basics will you need to get started and bring food production into your own backyard? The actual set up of your system will vary greatly depending its size and the space where you're setting it up, but here are some of the essentials:

An energy efficient pump. One pump is needed to move water from the fish tank to the grow bed. Water then can be returned to the fish through the tubing by gravity flow.

A tank for your fish and a grow bed medium with hydroponic components. A grow bed is the vessel you put your plants in. Red Scoria is a type of grow bed that is frequently used. Be sure to rinse it thoroughly before use so that it doesn't harbor ammonia or clog the system.

Tubing to transport water to and from grow beds. You can either use a constant flow or an ebb and flow system. The constant flow system produces lower dissolved oxygen at the root zone, so you'll need some aeration -- the circulation of air to increase oxygen levels of the water in the fish tank. You'll also have to remove solids such as fish waste and extra feed that isn't filtered out by the gravel. However, a constant flow system can enhance ammonia levels in the water, allowing for better nitration and higher growth rates. The ebb and flow system, on the other hand, improves oxygen at the root zone and saves energy because water doesn't have to be pumped constantly. Basically, you'll need to choose a system based on the nutritional requirements of the type of fish you're raising and the plants you're growing.

An aquatic water heater controlled by a thermostat to maintain water temperature in the system. Depending on the fish and plants you're cultivating, you'll want to maintain a temperature of between 70 and 86 degrees Fahrenheit (21 and 30 degrees Celsius).

Clay or gravel for grow bed. While the bottom of the plants' roots hang in the water, the plants themselves rest in a clay or gravel grow bed medium that helps to filter the water. These materials offer plant support, produce high plant growth yield, offer optimal water buffering and act as a biofilter.

Test kits to check the pH of water in the system. The optimal pH level in a system is 6.7 to 6.9.

On both a small and large scale, aquaponics definitely offers an environmentally beneficial way to cultivate fish and plants. For more information on aquaponics farming keep reading the below explanations.

BENEFITS OF AQUAPONICS

Problems with Organic certification:

Onceyou are certified, the inspector rarely stops by to check if you are truly practicing organic methods.

There iscurrently more organic produce being sold, than actually is being grown. Which means some produce labeled as organic is not. Theonly way to combat this is to know the farm you are buying from.

Why Aquaponics Is Better Than Organic

1. Bottom Line: There is no cheating on this with aquaponics, because we can't usechemical pesticides of any kind or our fish would die, period.

2. Even most approved organic pesticides would kill our fish. The fish act as the"canary in the coal mine", and force the aquaponics farmer to be honest. Even our tap water in Bend containschloramine, which is an additive much like chlorine that would kill our fish.

3. Aquaponics mimics the natural symbiotic relationship between fish & plants.

4. Even traditional organic farms need to supplement their soil with fertilizers. These fertilizers can be bad for theover health of the soil and watershed.

5. We are located right next to downtown Bend. You can come visit usand see how we grow

and treat our plants and fish, to be sure that what your eating is 100% chemical free!

6. No G.M.O. We do not grow any G.M.O. plants.

7. Another advantage of growing indoors is that we don't have to worry about sprays

from farms next door blowing in the wind over on toour crops. Or mysterious G.M.O. plants appearing in our crops like what happened in Eastern Oregon.

Other Benefits Of Aquaponics

Farming Technique

1. Our proprietary system grows six times more per square foot than traditional farming.

2. Aquaponics uses 90% less water than traditional farming.

3. With our system, we can grow any time of year, in any weather, anywhere on the planet.

4. Because aquaponics recycles the water in the system, we can grow in droughts and areas with little water.

5. Less pests to deal with since we are growing indoors.

6. There's no weeding!

7. Plants Grows Twice As Fast! Due to the naturally fortified water from the fish.

8. For the commercial farmer, aquaponics produces two streams of income, fish and veggies, rather than just one.

9. Our aquaponics farm does NOT require farmland with fertile soil, or even land with soil; aquaponics can be done just as successfully on sand, gravel, or rocky surfaces, which could never be used as conventional farmland.

10. Because we hang our grow lights vertically, and use both sides of the light (no reflector), our lights are twice as efficient, as they are growing two areas of plants versus the standard one area.

Environmental

1. Water Conservation: aquaponics uses 90% less water than traditional farming. Water and nutrients are recycled in a closed-loop fashion which conserves water.

2. Aquaponics Protects Our Rivers & Lakes: No harmful fertilizer run off into the water shed. In efforts to maintain nutrient rich soil, farms have to use a lot of fertilizers, those excess fertilizers eventually make it the rivers, where there are countless harmful side effects.

3. Gas Conservation: "Food Miles" are greatly reduced. Our produce only travels less than five miles from farm to consumer.Only serving the local community reduces harmful gas emissions.

4. Energy Conservation: Even with grow lights, we use   less energy than conventional commercial farming! All energy used in

aquaponics is electrical, so alternate energy systems such as solar, wind, and hydroelectric can be used to power our farm.

5. Land Conservation: Our system grows six times more per square foot than traditional farming.

6. Also, by growing in abandoned warehouses, we are using structures that already exist, saving money, energy and other valuable resources.

Health & Nutrition

1. Our fertilizer is from cold blooded fish which do not carry the E. coli or Salmonella, unlike

2. fertilizers from warm blooded animals.

3. Fish are the fastest converter of plant protein to animal protein.

4. Fish have no growth hormones, no mercury, no antibiotics, No P.C.B.s

5. Our Plants have no antibiotics.

6. Produce tastes better than that purchased at the grocery store (because it is not shipped and stored for extended periods of time).

Compared to Hydroponics

1. With Hydro you have to continuously change out your water supply, because the

nutrient solution builds up salts and chemicals in the water. Not only is this wasting more water than aquaponics, it is also polluting the watershed.

2. Nutrient solutions for hydro are super expensive, where the fish in aquaponics can be fed worms, bugs and scraps from the plants.

3. Hydro revolves around a sterile environment, where aquaponics embraces all micro-organism as they each play an important part in the growing process. As such aquaponics tends to have less diseases and pest problems.

4. In hydroponics, you don't get to raise and harvest fish.

5. Hydroponic growers can use toxic chemicals to control pests.

HOW TO CREATE YOUR AQUAPONICS SYSTEM AND WHAT YOU NEED CREATING IT

An aquaponics system is a symbiotic marriage of plants and aquatic animals cultivated in a recirculating environment. There are various types of aquaponics systems used for growing vegetables or plants. Knowing how big you want your aquaponics system to be before you purchase it will allow you to set a budget. Read on to learn a little about the basic equipment needed for aquaponics systems.

Chapter 9: Fish Tanks And Stand Pipes And Tanks Stands

Aquaponics is a blend of aquatic animals living in an environment where they provide the nutrients for the plants or vegetables growing in the same water in which they live. To begin creating your aquaponics system, you will need to decide which fish and other fauna you would like to house and how many you need. They will need a tank to live in and the tank requires stand pipes. You will also need to position your tank on a steady area or stand.

Clarifiers

You will need clarifiers for your aquaponics system. These are highly recommended as the best way to remove solids from the culture water. They also assist with the de-nitrification process and remove ammonia and nitrates. They are responsible for removing almost all of the water in the recirculation system and they can be used many times over with just marginal replacement needed from flushing the system to remove any solids that get trapped.

Bio-filters

Keeping the water clean and balanced in your aquaponics system is essential to keep it running efficiently. Bio-filters are a great way of controlling water pollution by biologically degrading and processing pollutants. There are horizontal bio-filters and upright bio-filter tanks available as well as a range of other types.

Oxygen Systems

Because you are keeping fish in your aquaponics systems, you will need an excellent oxygen distribution system. This is one of the must-have features as this is highly intrinsic to the health and growth of the fish. It will distribute oxygen to an optimum level suitable for the fish you have in your system.

Pumps

You will need a pump (or multiple pumps, depending on your system set-up) and the pumps serve a very important purpose. They will pump the water around the system, allowing it to be cleaned as it goes through the bio-filter and will return the fresher, cleaner water to the tank for best results.

Sundries

There are other smaller items needed to get your new aquaponics system up, running and performing as you need it to. Pipes and tubes and other accessories will be required and the best place to find them is in a kit found at a specialist store on website. Learn as much as you can about how aquaponics work before you commit to buying a complete system.

Plants and Fish

You will want your aquaponics system to function well for both your plants and the aquatic creatures you want to live and grow in your system. Choose the right fish that support the plant environment for the best results.

What You Will Need

4 X4'x 1/4" pressure-treated plywood

Electric screwdriver

Galvanized screws

Drill

1/4-inch drill bit

Nylon screen

Plastic liners

Potting soil

Plant

Sander

Paint

Stencils

Ruler or tape measure

Saw

Pencil

You can buy a flower box at gardening centers, but it is just as easy to build one. Creating your own flower box is not only inexpensive and fun but allows you to customize it however you like. Choose the size, shape, and the type of material to make it your own original design. The following steps will walk you through a simple flower box construction.

Step 1 - Determining the Size of the Flower Box

Before you begin building any outdoor planter, you must determine the size. First, decide where you want the box to go or, if you are planning on making multiple boxes, where they will each be placed. Next, measure the length of the area where the flower box will be resting. Now, consider how wide you want the flower box to be and how deep. Another consideration is deciding the number of plants you plan to grow in each planter. For this example, we'll be making a flower box that is 10" long, 5" deep, and 4" wide.

Step 2 - Transferring Measurements

With your measurements done, you are ready to purchase the material to build the flower box. For informational purposes, cedar and untreated wood are both recommended as each can withstand exposure and natural elements. Pressure-treated lumber is not recommended as the chemicals within the lumber that may be harmful to the plants and vegetables. Once you buy the plywood being used for this example, transfer the measurements to the material. First, use your ruler and carefully draw out the following dimensions (we'll be using our example measurements):

2 10-inch long by 5-inch wide pieces (Long Sides)

1 10-inch long by 4-inch wide piece (Bottom)

2 5-inch long by 4-inch wide (Short Sides)

Step 3 - Cutting and Preparing the Pieces

Now comes the more delicate part of the project. First, use a tape measure to measure each dimension then use a pencil to mark where you'll make the cut(s). Next, use your saw and begin cutting out all the pieces, then sand them down to remove any rough edges and imperfections. Now, test fit each of the pieces together to see if they are a good fit. Continue on otherwise sand the pieces again until they make a nice fit.

Step 4 - Assembling the Flower Box

With the dry run completed you can now assemble the flower box. This is where the drill, drill bit, galvanized screws, and screwdriver come into play.First, lay your bottom panel down then attach the long side panels to it.Next, attach the short ends to the flower box. Finally, drill five rows of three small holes each in the bottom of the flower box, which will be used for drainage. Cut and place a piece of vinyl or nylon screen along the bottom of the planter and secure with small nails. The screen serves as a protective liner to the wood. Last, use a sander to sand down any rough edges.

Step 5 - Customizing the Flower Box

Now you can customizeyour flower box. First, paint the box anycolor you want but useexterior paint unlessyour flower box will be inside. Next, usestencilsor a fine paintbrush to make designson the outside of the flower box. You can alsoantique the box with white paint, scuffing it with sandpaper and a hammer. Do not paint, prime, or stain the insideof theplanter as the mineralsand chemicals in paint can damage plants.

Step 6 - Planting

If you want to keep your plants in thestore containers you can simply place them in the flower box but if not, then read on. First, line the flower box with plastic planter liners that you havecut and trimmed. Next, line the bottom of theplanter with gravel tosupport drainage then fill theplanter halfway with potting soil. Now, transplant your plant from thestorecontainer to the flower box. Next, cover the roots with about an inch of potting soil. Finally, water the plant and enjoy them as they add beauty toyour home.

Chapter 10: Understanding Biological Surface Area In Aquaponics

Growing with aquaponics can be a fantastic way to experience higher yields, better efficiency and healthier plants.

To function well, aquaponic systems depend on a complex and robust ecosystem to cycle nutrients and create balance between organisms and their environment.

One aspect of this type of production method that often gets overlooked is biological surface area (BSA) in aquaponics.

This post is to help you better understand the importance of biological and specific surface area to produce higher yields and fewer frustrating mistakes!

What Is Biological Surface Area?

To start, biological surface area (BSA) is the amount of surface area inside your system that on which microbes can live. BSA is very important in aquaponic systems because these microbes are the engines of a healthy aquaponics system.

Microbes oxidize ammonia, assist in nitrification and mineralize materials like iron in order to foster healthy plant growth and a healthy system overall.

Measuring Biological Surface Area

We typically measure BSA in the total number of square feet per system.

o fully grasp this measurement, we'll also need to understand how much specific surface area (SSA) is our system. SSA is measured as the number of square feet per cubic foot (ft2/ft3).

This is the amount of square feet there are inside of the volume of media you're using.

Once we have calculated the specific surface area, all we have to do is multiply the SSA by the VOLUMEof the grow beds or ZipGrow Towers to get the Biological Surface Area.

For example...

Say you have a 700 square foot greenhouse. Leaving 30% space for access and maintanence, you're left with 500 square feet of growing space. Let's look at two growing systems within that space: one using ZipGrow Towers with Matrix Media (SSA 290 square feet per cubic foot) and one using media beds with pea gravel (SSA 85 square feet per cubic foot).

You'll see that in terms of BSA, the two systems are a bit different. Another factor that you have to keep in mind, however, is how much of growing space you have per square foot of BSA. (This is your space use efficiency ratio, which we talk about more in this book.)

Why Understanding Biological Surface Area Is Important

Figuring out how much BSA is in your system will help you to understand whether or not your fish are understocked or overstocked and help you make the adjustments necessary for a efficient, effective growing system.

To give you an idea of how much BSA/SSA is in various media types, I'll turn it over to Dr. Nate Storey's research on the matter.

From Storey, 2012:

Table 2.01 Specific surface area comparisons for different substrates.

Particle SizeSpecific Surface Area

Media Typeinchesmmft2 ft-3m-2m-3Void Ratio (%)Hydraulic Conductivity (m/d)

Medium Sand0.123270886401

Pea Gravel0.5714.58528028104

Rock125216940105

Large Rock4102123948106

Plastic biofilter media1258528090107

Plastic biofilter media2504815793108

Plastic biofilter media3.5893812595108

ZipGrow Matrix mediaN/AN/A29096091107*

* estimated to be approximately that of small diameter plastic biofilter media

As you can see, different medias have drastically different biological surface areas.*

"These studies are especially relevant to this research, and especially the design phase of Tower development, during which the properties of the media used had to be closely defined. Deciding on the media type was difficult and literature detailing the inverse relationship between particle size and Specific Surface Area (SSA in m2 m-3) was useful. This is due to the relationship between percolation and SSA that is a feature of most aggregates. As particle size gets smaller, specific surface area for that media type increases, that is to say, the surface area to volume ratio increases, i.e.:

- medium sand (3 mm diameter), SSA= 886 m2 m-3;

- pea gravel (14.5 mm diameter), SSA=280 m2 m-3;

- medium gravel (25 mm diameter), SSA=69 m2 m-3;

- large gravel (102 mm diameter), SSA=39 m2 m-3; (Crites, et al., 2006).

It should be noted that values in the literature can be somewhat contradictory depending on the source. This is primarily due to differences in measurement and classification standards. What these values will show however, regardless of technique, is that smaller particles are better suited for integration into systems where high SSA values are important.

Unfortunately, the reality is that these small particles trap solids much more efficiently and rapidly foul with accumulated biosolids, leading to anerobic conditions and lower dissolved oxygen (DO) concentrations that negate the benefits of small particle size. This low hydraulic conductivity and small pore size (low void space/void fraction) makes small-particle media inappropriate for most biologically active systems with active cycling. To avoid this problem, larger particle sizes are commonly used (17 mm crushed granite or ¾ inch crushed granite) having higher void ratios (and resulting high hydraulic conductivity) so that solids impact percolation less. However, even though these crushed aggregates have significantly higher SSA than non-angular and non-crushed aggregates, SSA is still comparatively low, resulting in reduced overall system Biological Surface Area (BSA or total surface area of system measured in m2)."

CALCULATING YOUR BSA

Remember: as an absolute minimum, your system needs at least:

2.5 ft2 of BSA/gallon of water (at low stocking densities and low feeding rates)

For a healthier system, we would recommend:

10 ft2/gallon of water OR 100 ft2/pound of fish

EXAMPLE:

If you're stocking fish at 1 pound per 10 gallons, for every pound of fish, you'll need 25 ft2 of BSA - This will be the amount you'll need for adequate waste and ammonia processing.

Does The Age Of My System Matter?

Yes!

Generally speaking, older systems are going to be much more efficient at processing waste (i.e. the microbial communities inhabiting older systems are much more established, stable and able to operate more effectively as a result).

Younger systems (see: newer/less mature systems), you'll need more BSA right away to help in the nitrification process.

** IMPORTANT: If you haven't properly cycled your system, it doesn't matter how much biological surface area you have.**

Remember: A truly healthy AP system requires as much Biological Surface Area as possible - BSA is the horsepower of your aquaponics system!

Zipgrow Towers & High Specific Surface Area

If you noticed in the table above, ZipGrow Towers have a very high SSA, BSA and void ratio.

The reason for this is that they were designed this way!

As you see in the table, our Towers and Matrix Media have 290 square feet of specific surface area per cubic foot of our media.

Our media fibers provide a ton of surface area for our microbes to hang out on and keep our system healthy.

The high SSA, in combination with a void ratio of 91%, which allows water and solids to flow through our Towers easily, creates a productive powerhouse in our aquaponics system. (Don't forget the light weight and ease of transport/maintenance!)

This media and ZipGrow Towers are available to anyone on online stores.

RECOMMENDED PLANTS AND FISH IN AQUAPONICS

The fish and plants you select for your aquaponic system should have similar needs as far as temperature and pH. There will always be some compromise to the needs of the fish and plants but, the closer they match, the more success you will have.

As a general rule, warm, fresh water, fish and leafy crops such as lettuce and herbs will do the best. In a system heavily stocked with fish, you may have luck with fruiting plants such as tomatoes and peppers.

Fish that we have raised in aquaponics with good results:

tilapia

blue gill/brim

sunfish

crappie

koi

fancy goldfish

pacu

various ornamental fish such as angelfish, guppies, tetras, swordfish, mollies

Other fish raised in aquaponics:

carp

barramundi

silver perch, golden perch

yellow perch

Catfish

Large mouth Bass

Plants that will do well in any aquaponic system:

any leafy lettuce

pak choi

kale

swiss chard

arugula

basil

mint

watercress

chives

most common house plants

Plants that have higher nutritional demands and will only do well in a heavily stocked, well established aquaponic system:

tomatoes

peppers

cucumbers

beans

peas

squash

broccoli

cauliflower

cabbage

These are of the other crops that Nelson and Pade, Inc.® has grown in aquaponics:

bananas

dwarf citrus trees: lemons, limes and oranges

dwarf pomegranate tree

sweet corn

micro greens

beets

radishes

carrots

onions

edible flowers: nasturtium, violas, orchids

The 9 Best Fish For Aquaponics And How To Buy Them

Aquaponics has become increasingly popular as a growing system in the past 10 years. It combines conventional aquaculture with hydroponics to form a highly sustainable and environmentally responsible method of Agriculture.

Aquaponic systems come with many benefits – very low water consumption as compared to traditional agricultural means, low energy usage, little to no chemical usage, low susceptibility to pests and diseases, and it's environmentally friendly with no waste or biproduct.

Setting up an aquaponic system comes with its challenges. The four main components – a grow bed, a tank, fish, and plants, should be carefully planned out. The grow bed is used in raising plants in the aquaponic system. The tank is where fish will be kept – you will have to consider the size of the aquaponic system when deciding the size of the tank.

Fish play a key role in an aquaponic system, as they will be the source of natural fertilizer for the plants being cultivated. Plants also play a key role, taking up waste left by the fishes and converting them to rich nutrients.

To build a successful aquaponic system, you will also have to carefully select the fish by considering several factors. It is important to plan which types of vegetables you want to grow and pair them with the right type of fish. Certain fish and plants thrive at specific temperatures and pH levels so it is essential to make sure that both plants and fish will be successful in the given water conditions.

What Are The Best Species Of Fish To Use For My Aquaponics System?

Tilapia

Edible

Omnivorous

70-80 degrees F

pH level 7-8

Breed every 4-6 weeks

Require energy source to maintain water temperature

Great for beginners

Tilapia originated in the wild in Africa and in the Nile River Basin of Lower Egypt and are considered to be one of the oldest farmed fish on the planet. Among the most popular species for an aquaponics system especially for beginners, it has also taken third place as one of the most important fish in aqua-culture, after carp and salmon. Their high protein content, large size, rapid growth and palatability have made them favorable. Tilapia are also one of the easiest and most profitable fish to far due to their omnivorous diet, tolerance of high stocking densities and rapid growth. They prefer water with a pH level between 7-8.

The Nile Tilapia and Mozambique Tilapia are two of the most favored types of Tilapia due to their fast growth rate and late breeding stage.

Tilapia are durable fish that are resistant to parasites and diseases making them an excellent fish for beginners. They can also tolerate wider range of water quality and temperature changes. They thrive in water temperatures between 70-80 degrees F and are usually kept at around 73 degrees to accommodate the plants. They're easy to breed and grow quite quickly – up to 2.5 lbs. in 7 months.

One thing to consider is that Tilapia can breed almost too efficiently – spawning every 4-6 weeks so a second tank might be helpful in containing the babies.

Tilapia can be quite costly to maintain as famers need an energy source to maintain a tropical temperature range in their tanks as they require warm water.

Perch

Edible

Carnivorous

67 to 77 degrees F

pH level 6.5 to 8.5

Breeds once a year

Perch are a great choice for aquaponic system because of their taste, hardiness, growth rate and nutrition. Perch are better at retaining omega 3 than any other fish when fed with feeds high in omega-3 oils. Perch will not breed in captivity, but they have a fast growth rate.

There are three main perch species: the European Perch – found in Europe and Asia, the Balkhash perch – found in Kazakhstan, Uzbekistan, and China, and the yellow perch also found in the US and Canada.

The yellow perch, in particular, are best for aquaponics due to their moderate temperature range and wide pH range. Thriving in temperatures between 67 and 77 degrees F, these carnivorous fish typically reach about 15 inches in size and 2.2 lbs. in weight.

They have the widest pH range of 6.5 and 8.5 among the aquaponic fish species. Perch only breed once a year and require and sudden change in temperature from cold to warm as to simulate the change from winter to spring.

Trout

Edible

Carnivorous

55 to 65 degrees F

pH level 6.7 to 7.7

Requires large tank for optimum growth

Requires oxygen level of at least 5.5mg/L

Trout are closely related to salmon and char and are one of the most widely farmed fish in the world due to them being fairly easy to culture. Most trout live in freshwater lakes and rivers, while others live out their live out their lives in fresh water or spend two or three years at sea before returning to fresh water to spawn. They generally feed on other fish, and soft bodied aquatic invertebrates such as flies and dragonflies. They may also feed on shrimp and small animal parts. Unlike tilapia, trout will not handle dirty water.

Trout are somewhat bony, but the flesh is generally considered to be tasty. The flavor of the flesh is heavily influenced by the diet of the fish.

Among the three most common types of trout – brown, rainbow, and brook – rainbow trout make the best species for aquaponics due to their hardiness. Rainbow trout can withstand the varying conditions an aquaponics system will present.

They are considered a cold water fish and thrive in temperatures between 55 and 65 degrees F. They require a pH range between 6.7 and 7.7.

Trout can grow to about 15 inches in 9 months but require a large lank for them to grow in. Also, they require an oxygen saturation of at least 5.5mg/L. Stocking density is something to pay close attention to so as to make sure that there's adequate oxygen for all the fish.

Largemouth Bass

Edible

Carnivorous

65 to 75 degrees F

pH level 6.5 to 8.5

Can grow up to 12 lbs.

Requires large tank for optimum growth

Keep away from bright light

Bass, a popular American game fish, are very hardy and can tolerate low water temperatures. Bass eat worms, insects, larvae as well as high protein pellets. They prefer to feed on food that stays in the surface or that sinks slowly, rather than to feed off the bottom of the tank.

There are many species of Bass to choose from. These are among the most popular for aquaponics:

Hybrid striped bass which are well suited to aquaponics as they are hardy and resilient to extremes of temperatures and to low dissolved oxygen.

Smallmouth bass which are carnivorous and eat crayfish, insects and smaller fish. They can tolerate cool water but are reluctant to eat pelleted food

Largemouth bass – The northern strain and the Florida strain is generally larger and lives much longer.

Australian bass which are small to medium sized. They feed on insects, or on protein rich pellets.

Though not considered a beginner species for aquaponics by any means, Largemouth bass are widely used in aquaponics systems due to their potential for growth. A full sized adult largemouth bass can reach 12 lbs. in weight in 16 months.

Largemouth bass do not like bright light. They require a strict feeding regime of small shrimp and insects as a baby and then snails and crayfish as an adult. They require a steady water temperature between 65 to 75 degrees and prefer a pH level of 6.5 to 8.5.

Though much maintenance is require for largemouth bass, their size and hearty meat provide a very rewarding harvest.

Catfish

Edible

Omnivorous

75 to 85 degrees F

pH level 7 to 8

Can tolerate wide range of water conditions

Good choice for beginners

Catfish are one of the most farmed types of fish and are sought after for their taste - their meat is consumed as a delicacy around the world. Catfish are omnivorous bottom feeders and valuable scavengers. As they are a strong fish, they can withstand a wide range of water conditions. They are not territorial and can tolerate a higher stocking density. Catfish are easy to breed and grow, and within 3 months can be harvested for cooking.

Catfish thrive in a similar temperature range as tilapia at 75 to 85 degrees F and have a pH range of 7 to 8. They grow fast and can reach 2-3 lbs. in 12 months.

Barramundi

Edible

Carnivorous

77 to 86 degrees F

pH level 6.5 to 7.2

Special care needed for fingerlings

Grows extremely fast

Delicious and extremely nutritious

Barramundi is an excellent table fish highly regarded in most restaurants and a great fish for Aquaponics, but it is not recommended for beginners. They prefer warm water are reputed to be fast growers.

However, they are hard to grow as Barramundi fingerlings need to be graded to survive. The fingerlings attack and eat one another – the larger sized fish will nip and wound the smaller fish. The wounded smaller fish will eventually die if not eaten by the others. Barramundi need lots of dissolved oxygen going into their tank and they need very good quality water.

Chapter 11: Resilient In Different Water Conditions

Carp are a species of oily freshwater fish, native to Asia. Various species of carp can be reared as food. They are omnivorous and can feed on algae, plants, insects and many other soft bodied aquatic invertebrates. Carp have good reproductive capabilities and can easily adapt in various environments.

Over the past few year, the demand for carp in Western Europe has declined as more desirable table fishes, trout and salmon, have become more available through extensive farming. Nevertheless, Carp make a good species for aquaponics due to their resilience to changes in water conditions.

They have a temperature range of 80 to 82 degrees F and a pH range of 7.5 to 8.0.

Koi

Non-edible

Omnivorous

65 to 78 degrees F

pH levels 6.5 to 8.0

Great for beginners

Highly successful in aquaponics due to hardiness

Resistant to most disease and parasites

Koi are one of the most popular fish used in aquaponics. They have a long lifespan and can easily live and breed within the aquaponic system. Koi are also fairly disease and parasite resistant. They are omnivores and can eat just about any food. As they eat algae, debris and plant matter that fall into their pond, additional feeding may not be necessary. Waste production will have to be monitored and a large and more efficient filter may need to be installed.

Koi are not considered to be a good fish for eating, so you will have to seek alternatives.

They thrive in temperatures of 65 to 78 degrees F and pH levels of 6.5 to 8.0.

They are highly successful among beginners due to their adaptability and resilience.

Goldfish

Inedible

Omnivorous

65 to 78 degrees F

pH levels 6.5 to 8.0

Goldfish are an ideal aquaponics fish as they produce and eat a large amount of excretion, thus providing plenty of nitrates for the plants. They are also hardy, depending on which species you select. However, rapid changes in temperature can be fatal.

There are generally two types of goldfish — twin-tailed and single-tailed. Be mindful to avoid mixing these two species together as twin-tailed fish could end up suffering greatly. As single-tailed gold fish have slim bodies, and are more aggressive and faster swimmers, twin-tailed gold find it hard to compete with them.

Goldfish are inedible ornamental fish and thrive in temperatures of 65 to 78 degrees F and pH levels of 6.5 to 8.0.

How And Where To Purchase Fish Online

Online transactions have revolutionized how we purchase items and live fish are no exception. Yes, it is possible to have live fish shipped to your door by a reputable company via expedited shipping and proper packaging. Here are some tips in ensuring you have ahassle-free buying experience.

Select a Reputable Vendor - Be sure to read the reviews posted by other customers and ensure that the vendor is reliable in their packaging and delivery of the live fish. Make sure the fish they are selling are healthy and well.

Look for Guarantee - Only purchase from stores that offer a guarantee that their fish will arrive alive and will offer a refund for any other outcome.

Expedited Shipping Only - Most reputable online fish vendors will only sell ship the fish under expedited or next day service due to the time-sensitive packaging, but it doesn't hurt to double check for it.

Be Home When it Arrives - Expedited shipping is great in ensuring that it arrives at your doorstep on time but it doesn't help if the package is sitting on your front porch while you're on vacation. Be sure that someone is home to place the fish in their proper conditions right away to ensure optimum health.

What To Consider When Choosing Fish Species For Your Aquaponic System

Ornamental vs Edible Fish

Your choices of fish will depend on whether you want to eat them. As the name suggests, you should choose edible fish if you're looking to grow fish that you can eat.

The inedible fishes Koi and Goldfish do have their own benefits. Goldfish, while slightly more difficult to maintain than Koi, are much less expensive and can be used for smaller aquaponics systems or trial runs. Koi fish are great for beginner systems as they're quite resilient to the volatility a a new aquaponics system can present. They're also very resistant to diseases and parasites, two things that can turn a well-maintained aquaponic system upside-down.

Edible fishes have the obvious benefit and the larger, faster-growing fish come with their own special conditions and requirements.

Breeding, Growth Rate, And Stocking Density

Breeding is a factor to consider when purchasing fish and when considering the type of system set-up as a whole. Some species don't reproduce easily in a controlled tank which can be frustrating, especially for beginners. Others, such as Tilapia and Catfish breed quite quickly, which can also lead to complications if the system isn't built properly for it.

Spawning vs Livebearing - There are two main methods fish use for breeding – spawning and live-bearing. Most fish spawn, whereas a fair number of fish are livebearers. Spawning involves reproducing freely by laying eggs when special conditions, known as spawning triggers, are met. Live-bearing involves retaining eggs inside the body and live birth to free-swimming young. Livebearers are generally preferred for fish-breeding. Live-bearing aquarium fish, often simply called livebearers, are fish that retain the eggs inside the body and give birth to live, free-swimming young.

Growth Rate - The growth rates of fish vary. With your aquaponic system, it is better to have fish with a range of growth rates to harvest fish regularly over a long period of time. The range of fish growth rates vary. It is also important to consider the time of year at which the fish are ready to be harvested.

Overcrowding is an issue that needs to be addressed as we'll see in the next section.

Population Density - You will have to stock your tank in with a reasonable number of fish, keeping in mind the growth rate of the fish, the available space in the tank and your budget for purchase and maintenance. The size your fish could grow up to should also be kept in mind when considering the available space. An overcrowded fish tank can disrupt the oxygen and ammonia levels in the water, as can an underpopulated tank. Keep population density in mind when harvesting fish as well.

Fish Diet

In terms of diet, fish can be classified into three main categories – herbivore, carnivore or omnivore. Fish suitable for aquaponic systems are either carnivore or omnivore.

Carnivores require a high protein diet which can be difficult to achieve without purchasing high-quality commercial feed specifically formulated for carnivorous fish. Some carnivorous fish may prefer to feed on other fishes instead, especially the young and weak. So generally, carnivores cannot be mixed with other species and they should all be of approximately same sizes to prevent them from snacking on each other.

Omnivores can coexist with their own species and with other omnivorous fish species, so they are an excellent choice for a community tank. Omnivores are also known to be the easiest to feed.

Maintenance Difficulty

You will need to maintain your aquaponic system by testing the water, changing the water and checking your equipment, but your fish will also need some maintenance. Some fish are difficult to care for whereas others are relatively easier. Your fish may fall ill or experience bullying, resulting in you having to administer medication to your fish or put your fish in isolation.

Temperature

Fish are cold-blooded animals – they take on the temperature of the water in which they live in, so temperature plays a very important role. The water temperature requirements of fish depend on their natural climate.

For example, fish originating in the lake waters of Africa such as tilapia have evolved to thrive in warm water (above 70oF), whereas fish originating in streams of North America such as trout have evolved to thrive in cold water (55oF and below). So, when choosing your fish, you should be mindful about what water temperature you will be able to provide.

The fish and plants you select for your aquaponic system should also have similar needs in terms of temperature. The closer they match, the higher the chances of success of your aquaponic system.

Chapter 12: Hydroponics Vs Aquaponics Which Is Better

There has been many debates as to which method of gardening would come out on top in a battle of hydroponics vs aquaponics.

In this article, we'll be looking at the main differences between the two and if aquaponics really is the best of both worlds of hydroponics and aquaculture.

What Is Hydroponics?

Hydroponics uses only water and chemical nutrients to cultivate plants, without the necessity of soil. It's not only the main production method of much of the greenhouse tomato, basil and lettuce grown in North America, but it's also popular among marijuana growers.

The advantages of using hydroponics to grow plants are:

No soil is necessary.

It's stable and produces high yields.

There is no damage from pesticides.

The controlled system means that no nutrition pollution is released into the environment.

Lower nutrient requirements due to control over nutrient levels.

Lower water requirement as water stays in the system and can be reused.

The Differences Between Hydroponics & Aquaponics

Hydroponics and aquaponics share a few similarities. They both use nutrient-rich water that's highly oxygenated to bathe the plants' roots continuously, and in both systems, plants see better growth rates in comparison with those that are grown in soil.

Although aquaponics borrows many techniques from hydroponics such as their NFT (nutrient film technique) and DWC (deep-water culture), there are many significant differences where aquaponics improves upon.

Cost Of Chemical Nutrients – In a hydroponics system, chemical nutrients used to feed plants are expensive and costs are gradually rising due to over-mining and scarcity. In an aquaponics system, fish feed is used instead which is not only cheaper, but will provide you with bigger as well as support for plants.

Retain Nutrient Solution – Certain periods, water in hydroponic systems needs to be unloaded because of the build-up of salts and chemicals to the point where levels become toxic to plants. Where the waste water is disposed of needs to be carefully considered, but in an aquaponic system, there's a natural balance of nitrogen and water is never replaced, only topped up due to evaporation.

Productivity – It has been shown in several studies and research that once the aquaponic biofilter is fully established (after a period of 6 months), an aquaponic gardener will generally see quicker and more efficient results in terms of plant growth compared to hydroponics.

Ease Of Maintenance – An aquaponic system is much easier to maintain since there's no need to check the electrical conductivity once everyday as you would have to in a hydroponic system. The natural ecosystem in aquaponics means that elements have a tendency to balance each other out, and you would only need to check pH and ammonia levels once a week, and nitrate levels once a month.

Organic Growth – Hydroponics is made up of a sterile man-made environment while aquaponics is a replication of a natural ecosystem, thus making it completely organic. Hydroponic systems use costly nutrients made up of a mixture of chemicals and salts to feed plants, but in an aquaponic system, plant food is made from the conversion of solid fish waste by bacteria and composting worms. This natural process results in better plant growth and lower disease rates.

NATURAL PEST CONTROL

Natural pest control is an important consideration when it comes to establishing and maintaining an aquaponics system. Keeping your aquaponic system organic is one way to make sure the plants, fish, and food you harvest are safe and edible. Too many chemicals can be dangerous to both the fish and the people working with them. Studies have also shown a strong correlation between chemicals in the food system and many illnesses and diseases. With this in mind, you will want to find a safe but effective form of natural pest control. To do this, you need to know your enemy pests, understand common organic techniques for repelling or eliminating pests, and how beneficial bugs can work wonders in your aquaponic garden.

Aquaponic Pests

In an aquaponic system, pests can be just as big of a problem as they are for other gardening or farming methods. This is especially true of outdoor or backyard setups although it can be an issue indoors as well. Aquaponic pests are no different from your common garden pests, and they can cause some serious damage to your plants and the flowers, fruits, or vegetables they produce. Some of the worst insect offenders are:

Aphids

Caterpillars Tomato Hornworms

Colorado Potato Beetles

Mealybugs

Cutworms

Squash Vine Borers

Squash Bugs

Various plant-eating beetles

These insects can wipe our your entire crop if not handled properly, but using pesticides can be a real problem in an aquaponic system, even if organic gardening is not your focus. The harsh chemicals and poisons found in most pesticides can be extremely dangerous to your fish.

So how do you stop insects from destroying your plants while keeping your fish safe? You do it with proven organic gardening methods. There are plenty of well-documented ways to safely eliminate or reduce the number of pests that are attacking your plants. Begin by checking the plants regularly for pests. Hand removal will work wonders for visible pests you find on your plants. Just pick off and destroy any bugs you see. This is fairly labor intensive, so it is a good idea to use hand removal in conjunction with other methods. One popular method used in both aquaponics and traditional methods is the use of pest-repelling plants. Some plants just drive pests away, and you can plant them alongside the produce you want to grow. You can plant artemisias, nasturtiums, catnip, dill, chrysanthemums, chives, petunias, mint, and more as a form of natural pest control.

Another simple organic gardening method you can use in your aquaponic system is bug netting. This creates a physical barrier around the plants and will prevent many pests from getting in. This method works indoors and outdoors, but regular inspection of the plants is still strongly recommended. You can also look at non-pesticide methods of destroying the pest population. Glue traps are available and can be used throughout the grow beds of your aquaponic system to catch insects. The only drawback is these traps will catch insects that you want to have around like pollinators and other beneficial bugs. This brings us to another common technique for eliminatingpests that you can use, beneficial insects.

Beneficial Insects

Bringing some insects that prey on plant-damaging species into your aquaponic system is an excellent method of organic pest control. There are several insect varieties that would be more than happy to make a meal out of the pests that are munching on your plants. You can attract these beneficial varieties by creating a nice habitat for them. Most of the species that eat garden pests are easily attracted by flowers. In some cases, particularly with indoor systems, you may need to give nature a hand by adding the helpful insect species yourself. You can purchase pest-munching insects or find them yourself outdoors and bring them into your system. Some beneficial insects that are an excellent form of natural pest control for your aquaponic system include:

Ladybugs/Lady Beetles – Both the adult and larval forms of these little guys can work wonders when it comes to destroying garden pests. They eat aphids, smaller beetles and caterpillars, and most insect eggs. Some species even eat mealybugs, mites, and other soft-bodied insects. They can even devour powdery mildew, which is another common problem in aquaponic systems.

Lacewings – The larvae of the lacewing eat just about everything from aphids to caterpillars to mealybugs. They are also quite fond of insect eggs and other larvae. Adults of the species are also known to eat other insects, although their preferred food is nectar.

Spiders – Although not technically an insect, these creatures are great at keeping pest populations under control. Even young or smaller spiders can do a great job of eating up insects that destroy your plants. Anything that finds its way into their web, including caterpillars, aphids, moths, cutworms, squash bugs, and budworms.

Tachinid Flies – Their larvae can devour caterpillars, cutworms, squash bugs, beetles, earwigs, and even grasshoppers. The adults have also been known to eat other insects, but generally prefer nectar and pollen, making them excellent pollinators too.

Ground Beetles – The adults of this species are fairly large, and just one can eat quite a few garden pests. They will help keep slugs and snails, cutworms, caterpillars, potato beetles, squash vine borers, root maggots, and budworms under control. Soldier Beetles are another similar species that offer the same benefits.

With a little effort, it is entirely possible to keep bugs from destroying your aquaponic plantswithout doing any harm to your fish or yourself in the process. Avoiding pesticides and focusing on natural pest control methods will help ensure the success of your aquaponic system. You can keep damaging insects out of your garden with preventative methods like planting pest-repelling plants or using nets or traps.You can also employ some beneficial bugs that will help keep the damaging insects under control by eating them. By using a combination of these methods, you will be able to keep your system running smoothly and reap a healthy harvest.

How To Use Pesticides In Aquaponics Without Hurting Your Fish

The use of pesticides in aquaponics is a very touchy subject, and we've seen both the good and bad side of pesticide use in aquaponic systems. There are many opinions on pesticide use, all with varying degrees of validity. No matter what they say, however, all of these opinions boil down to a single fact:

Chemical pest management in aquaponic systems must be approached judiciously, thoughtfully and with caution, whether you are using a homemade remedy or a commercial product.

Before I begin to talk about the controls, you must know that this information was hard-won over the course of many years. Pests are inevitable in aquaponic systems, and dealing with them has always presented a dilemma for aquaponic producers, primarily because there are so few pesticides that are non-toxic, or of low toxicity to fish, but also because no one knew how much could be safely used. The team here led by Dr. Nate Storey has run a

quaponic systems using media beds, DWC, and ZipGrow Towers with various crops and fish types. We've killed a few fish, and have learned our lessons about pesticides in aquaponics through trial and error! We offer those lessons to you now. In this post, we're going to discuss:

Homemade vs commercial controls

Organic controls and IPM

Chemical control options for aquaponic systems

How to determine the danger of a given pesticide

Safely applying pesticides

How to tell if your fish have been affected by a pesticide

Let's talk about the options that you have for using pesticides in an aquaponic system.

Why We Rely On Commercial Products Over Homemade Remedies

Many aquaponic practitioners swear by garlic, chili, and vermicompost based concoctions, and to be fair, these can be effective on specific pests.Having tried almost all of the home remedies over the years, these days we rely entirely upon commercial products. As a commercial producer, we don't have the time or energy that homemade remedies require, nor the luxury of using marginally effective controls.This means that we use proven commercial products that have been studied and provide the information necessary to determine their effect on our aquaponic system products that we know from experience kill and control pests.

OMRI certified pesticides and IPM

We focus on organic pesticides, most of which are OMRI (Organic Materials Review Institute) certified.This is primarily because most commercial aquaponic producers grow "organic" produce and use pesticides permissible under USDA Organic Standards.Before we begin to discuss individual brands and products, I would first encourage you to do some research on integrated pest management, commonly referred to as IPM.

IPM is a pest control strategy that incorporates cultural, mechanical, chemical, and biological pest control into a larger context of economics, environment and human health. The rules of IPM promote a holistic view of pest control using compatible controls and eliminating unnecessary spraying.

For aquaponic producers IPM is important, not just because you are operating on a budget, (and IPM is the most cost-effective way to control pests) but because you have more complex environmental constraints than the average producer, and your customers are probably concerned about healthy food.Operating without an IPM strategy in place could make pest control unnecessarily expensive, impact your fish health and the health of your system, or impact the health of your customers.

Controls diversity is key to sustainability

In our farm, we use a combination of controls. It is important to maintain diversity in your control techniques to make sure that the pests in your greenhouse are not becoming resistant to the controls that you are using. I've met people that use a single control for many months, if not years on end. They always say, "It works great and I don't have any problems," and they might have good control, for a little while longer at least. But the unfortunate nature of greenhouse and garden pests is that they adapt very quickly to toxins in their environment, and rapidly become resistant to even the most toxic pesticides.Varying your control methods and incorporating chemical, biological, mechanical and cultural controls in tandem helps prevent resistance developing.

Pesticides in aquaponics Chemical controls:

We use a variety of products that exert chemical control over our greenhouse pests, including:

Pyrethrin based products (See Pyganic 1.4, Safer Endall Insecticidal soap, etc.)

Soaps (Safer products)

Azadirachtin based products (extracted from neem oil; see Azamax, etc.)

Neem oil and neem oil derivatives

Note: Pyrethrins are very toxic and can only be considered for use in systems with very little exposed water like ZipGrow Tower based systems.

Pesticide-needy crops & pesticide-sensitive fish can be an awkward match

In a perfect world, pests could be completely excluded from growing environments, and they would never become a problem. While some growers have come close to this goal, total exclusion is extremely difficult.

At one point or another, 99% of growers need to use pesticidal sprays.

The problem?Even if a spray is safe for humans, fish are wildly different from humans, and their close relationship with the water makes them vulnerable to any compounds there.

The intimate relationship created between fish and the water by diffusion through skin and gills means that they are extremely vulnerable to any component of the water.

Chapter 13: How Growers Know The Harmfulness

Of A Pesticide To Their Fish

Most pesticide labels list a characteristic called LC50. LC50 refers to the lethal concentration of a pesticide at which 50% of the tested population dies. The tested populations typically include some species of fish (often trout, Oncorhynchus spp., or tilapia, Oreochromis spp.). The LC50 for these species are what you want to pay attention to. If you can't find this on the label or SDS (Safety Data Sheet), then check out scientific studies (Google Scholar is a great place to start looking) on lethal concentration and that pesticide. Go with the lowest number listed.

To find this value, look up the label and/or SDS for the pesticide in question. They will often be listed together.

The SDS will have the LC50 listed. Here is the SDS for Serenade, for example.

Note that the LC50 value is listed within a certain time period. Use the shortest time period listed. (96 hours is fairly safe.)

Take the volume of your system in liters and multiply it by the LC50 value. That is the maximum amount of that pesticide that you can use.

Let's look at an example using pyrethrum (type 1 pyrethrin), the active ingredient in Pyganic 1.4.

When we look for this number we find that the most conservative LC listed is 0.0014 mg/L (96 hrs;Americamysis bahia). We need to determine how much pyrethrin is required to hit the LC50 for your system.

Step 1: Take 'the volume of your system in liters and multiply it by the LC50 (96 hr) value. We'll use the Bright Agrotech aquaponic system as an example.

(4,300 gal./sys.)(3.79 L/gal.) = (16,279 L/sys.)(0.0014 mg/L) = 22.79 mg/sys.

Step 2: Then we take the pyrethrin concentration and determine how much pyrethrin is being mixed and applied in the greenhouse.

The label recommends mixing 1–2 fluid ounces of Pyganic 1.4 with every gallon of water in compressed sprayers (what we use), which is between 2–4 Tbsp/gallon. In my greenhouse, the entire crop can be sprayed with 1.5 gallons of mix, which at the highest application rate is around 6 Tbsp (or 3 fluid ounces).

The label tells us that 0.05 lbs of active ingredient (pyrethrin) is the equivalent of 59 fluid ounces.

0.05 lbs pyrethrin/59 fluid ounces = 0.0008475 lbs pyrethrin/fluid ounce

0.0008475 lbs pyrethrin/fluid ounce * 453592 mg/lb = 384 mg pyrethrin/fluid ounce

3 fluid ounces/system * 384 mg pyrethrin/fluid ounce = 1152 mg pyrethrin/system

This number is much larger than the LC50 for the system.

How growers keeppesticides used out of the system water

The second part of using LC50 is keeping a pesticide out of the water. Even if you are using the LC50 very carefully, you always want to have contingency measures in place. If you apply pesticides correctly and keep water surfaces from pesticide exposure, you shouldn't even get close to your highest acceptable pesticide concentration in the system water.

1- Proper application of pesticides

Every pesticide has an application process on the label.This describes the highest concentrations, mixing instructions, proper safety precautions and clothing, etc. Pesticide labels are legal documents and must be followed! To use a pesticide in any way other than what is listed on the label is unlawful. If you have questions about how to apply a pesticide, seek advice from an extension agent, who is trained to dispense this type of advice.

Equipment set up is another factor important to keeping pesticide toxicities from occurring.

2- Proper equipment use and set up

Pesticide sprays generally can't get into the system water unless the water is exposed in the same area where spraying is taking place. Smart set up can reduce the amount of water surface exposed. For growers using media beds, Bato buckets, or DWC, it's tough to separate growing surfaces from water. You can't use more than 50% of the LC50 in these types of systems, and sometimes even that is a risk.For growers using NFT, ZipGrow, or any equipment with a covering or separator between plants and the media/water, this is pretty simple. The housing on the ZipGrow Tower, for example, already keeps the media safe from contact with pesticides much better than in a technique like DWC. You'll find that certain pesticides have LC50 values that are quite high. A few of our favorites for aquaponics are Azadirachtin products like Azamax and Botanigard

How to tell if your fish have been affected by a pesticide

If you're monitoring your system correctly (you should be checking on fish every time you're in your growing environment), you'll notice any changes in fish appearance and behavior. Fish illness is recognizable by various symptoms. If you're new to farming or just not sure what to look for, here are some general symptoms that indicate fish distress:

Slow and/or erratic movement. Fish are milling slowly, respond slower than usual to feed, or are erratic in their movements.

Wobbly swimming and/or convulsions. Fish seem to have lost control, swim at an unbalanced angle, wobble on their axis, or are bending and contracting their bodies.

Fin extension. Fish fins and gill cover are extended from their bodies.

Darkening and discoloration. Sometimes discoloration is only evident in muscles under the dorsal fin.If you harvest a fish and notice discoloration while butchering, this could be a sick fish.

White spots. White spots on the body of a fish are usually indicative of Ichthyophtirius, a common fish parasite, not pesticide toxicity.

Bloating and raised scales. Again, this is indicative of a disease called Dropsy, not pesticide toxicity.

Enflamed or disintegrating fins. A sign of fin rot.

Gulping air. This is typically a dissolved oxygen problem.

Death.

If you notice any of these in a fish or several, remove all of the affected fish first and quarantine them. It's wise to keep a small tank or bin around for this purpose.Stop all feeding and test ammonia levels. (It could be that you're just dealing with ammonia toxicity.)If you suspect that there is pesticide toxicity, you may have to do a partial water change. Depending on the severity of the toxicity, replace 30–50% of the tank water. This is going to shock your fish, because you're dramatically changing their living conditions. As much as possible, use replacement water that has been dechlorinated (or run through an RO filter) and which is the same temperature as the tank water. If you deal with toxicity, redo your LC50 calculations. Make sure that there aren't any other factors at play (like zinc toxicity or ammonia poisoning) before ruling it a pesticide problem.

Chapter 14: Hydroponics Vs Aquaponics Which Is Better?

Aquaponics Gardens : Take a little time before you are ready to grow aquaponics plants

An aquaponic garden is a very different way of growing plants than people are accustomed to, but they are very easy to set up and maintain. There are a number of things about this way of farming that people will have to learn and get used to. But after seeing the results it can produce and the simplicity of the system, it can become a life-changing experience for those interested in growing their own food.

Aquaponics has nothing to do with modifying plants or changing the way plants grow. The plants grow naturally and go through all the growth phases they would have if they were planted in the ground. The difference is the medium in which the plants are grown. With this system the plants have delivered water and nutrients directly to the roots, so that they have sufficient means to produce maximum growth.

With an abundance of oxygenated water and nutrients, plants can grow closer together, allowing a number of times as much plant growth in a certain amount of space. But a new system will take some time before it can be really productive. A newly designed system will be relatively sterile and will not support plants. It takes some time to collect fish waste in the water and for the colonies of bacteria that convert it into plant nutrients to settle.

The amount of time will depend on different variables, but about three months is a customary amount of time before an aquaponic system begins to mature and begins to support plants. A full term can take up to 12 months. If you plant your plants right away, they will probably die. But after a few weeks you may want to plant and see how they do it. Perhaps there are enough nutrients to support some plants, but do not expect them to do well before the system has matured.

You can grow plants earlier if you want to add additional fertilizers. You must be careful to select organic sources that are safe for the fish. For those who are impatient, that may be the way to go, but many people prefer to wait until things develop automatically.

Once your system is mature and has a good balance, it can productive for years without problems. With the low cost and simplicity of these systems, they are quickly becoming a very popular way to grow home grown vegetables and fish of garden quality.

Best Plants Suitable for Aquaponics System

An aquaponics system is now a new way of planting that produces 100% organic fruit or vegetables and does not need any earth at all. The fish in the aquarium and the plants on the breeding bed share a symbiotic relationship. Plants grow with the help of the eliminated waste from the fish and transport it to the system of the plants for photosynthesis. This is possible because the roots of the plants have contact with the water. On the other hand, fish grow with the air from the plants. With little effort to ensure this system, plants will certainly grow.

If you have your own aquaponics system, you need to know which materials are needed for this. One of the decisions you have to make is the choice of plants for aquaponics. There are actually many options to choose from. But the biggest factor that can influence your choice is the availability of plant seedlings or maybe seeds.

There are some options for the best plants for aquaponics:

They can be vegetables, flowers or water plants. For a small aquaponics system in homes it is expected that fewer plants are needed. If you use it as a home decor, you can let plants bloom flowers on the aquaponics. While others who like to harvest vegetables for their tables, they can plant cucumber, tomatoes and pumpkin.

These vegetables can be vines or not:

If it is a vine, that is not a problem. As soon as the roots can have a strong grip on the breeding bed, it can grow and cover the entire breeding bed. Moreover, beans or pool beans in particular are also great plants for aquaponics. Peas are also very suitable for this system. Lovers of fresh green leafy vegetables can also opt for lettuce and cabbage. In fact, these two have grown popularly in aquaponics. Legumes and spinach can also be planted here. For those who like to pick some pink and sweet strawberries in their backyard, they can also try to plant them in the aquaponics system. Berries are also very suitable.

These are just a few of your options when choosing which plant you want to grow in your aquaponics. You just have to keep in mind that the growth of these plants in the aquaponics system will largely depend on the type of fish feed.

Top plants for aquaponics systems: Plants Suitable for aquaponics

Points of attention when choosing aquaponics plants:

Your climate: you do not want to grow winter plants if you live in Mexico or warm plants if you live in Alaska. It is possible but we will come back to that later.

Geographic placement in your garden: direct / indirect sunlight, climbing plants, root plants … etc

growth / consumption rate.

Survival of the plant in extreme weather.

Pay attention to the climate of your city, is it hot? Or on the colder extremes? It is very different, trust me but if you live in a city with a moderate climate, it will be easier for you; you can choose "warm" aquaponics plants.

Warm crops:

Artichoke – Plant in autumn for the spring harvest

Cardoon – Plant in autumn for the spring harvest

Chives – Plant in autumn or spring

Garlic – In mild winter areas, plants in autumn

Parsley – In cold climates, plant in the spring.

Turnip – Winter cultivation in mild winter areas. Where the winters are cold, you plant for the summer harvest in early spring.

Parsnip – In cold winter areas, sow in late spring, harvest in autumn. In mild winter areas, sow in the fall for harvest in the spring.

Shallot – In mild climates, plants in autumn.bulbs in late spring and summer.In cold climates, plants in early spring.

Sludge – Sow the seeds in autumn; Transplanted at any time

Cold crops:

Beets

Brussels sprouts

Cabbage

Carrots

Cauliflower

Herbs

Horseradish

Onions

Potatoes

Radicchio

Sweet potatoes

Winter squash

Chapter 15: Plants That Can Be Grown With Aquaponics

There are a number of plants that can be grown with aquaponics. These are of different classes and types, making the whole system more versatile and better suited for a higher yield. The plants that thrive best in an aquatic environment are:

Cruciferous plants: the aquaponics system is most suitable for cruciferous plants. These include:

Broccoli

Skip

Cauliflower

Beans

Nightshades: the second category of plants with a great success in an aquaponics medium are the night flakes. These are:

Tomatoes

Capsicum and other pepper varieties

Eggplant

Herbs: In addition to the vegetables we have treated in the above two points, the aquaponics system is also very suitable for the cultivation of some herbs. These include:

Basil

Watercress

Coriander

Lemongrass

Parsley

Sage

Salad Variants: If you are someone who leads the healthy life and eat lots of salads to keep you fresh all day long, then aquaponics is your friend. This is because there are many types of vegetables, such as red salad onions, shallots, snow peas and tomatoes that can be grown in this way. Together with the cruciferous vegetables all these products can be perfect for those who want to live a healthier life.

Flowers for more gardening success: those who have grown plants in the aquaponics medium know very well that sometimes you have to add something to the environment to produce better products.

For this purpose, you can plant a variety of roses in your hydrated ecosystem. Roses are one of those plants that can help to increase your overall plant yield without depleting the essential nutrients in the aquatic ecosystem.

In addition, aquaponic roses can ensure that your home stays fresh and fragrant at all times.

In this time when market prices for vegetables continue to rise, growing your own vegetables is a good alternative. The aquaponics system is one of the best ways to grow certain types of plants because it includes plants and aquatic animals in an environment that is advantageous to both parties.

As a self-sustaining unit, this ecosystem is perfect for people who are looking for a way to reduce the cost of their groceries without compromising food quality. All in all, aquaponics is one of the most efficient and beneficial processes for growing your own vegetables.